discussion

&LESSON
STARTERS
2

FOR YOUTH GROUPS

THE *ideas* LIBRARY

THE IDEAS LIBRARY

Administration, Publicity, & Fundraising
Camps, Retreats, Missions, & Service Ideas
Creative Meetings, Bible Lessons, & Worship Ideas
Crowd Breakers & Mixers
Discussion & Lesson Starters
Discussion & Lesson Starters 2
Drama, Skits, & Sketches
Games
Games 2
Holiday Ideas
Special Events

discussion & LESSON STARTERS 2

FOR YOUTH GROUPS

THE ideas LIBRARY

Youth Specialties

Zondervan Publishing House

Grand Rapids, Michigan
A Division of HarperCollins Publishers

Discussion & Lesson Starters 2
Copyright © 1997 by Youth Specialties, Inc.

Youth Specialties Books, 1224 Greenfield Dr., El Cajon, CA 92021, are published by Zondervan Publishing House, 5300 Patterson Ave. S.E., Grand Rapids, MI 49530.

Unless otherwise noted, all Scripture quotations are taken from the *Holy Bible: New International Version* (North American Edition). Copyright © 1973, 1978, 1984 by International Bible Society. Used by permission of Zondervan Publishing House.

Ideas in this book have been voluntarily submitted by individuals and groups who claim to have used them in one form or another with their youth groups. Before you use an idea, evaluate it for its suitability to your own group, for any potential risks, for safety precautions that must be taken, and for advance preparation that may be required. Youth Specialties, Inc., and Zondervan Publishing House are not responsible for, nor have any control over, the use or misuse of any of the ideas published in this book.

Project editor: Vicki Newby
Cover and interior design: Curt Sell
Art director: Mark Rayburn
0-310-22033-5

Printed in the United States of America

00 01 02 03 04 05 06/ / 10 9 8 7 6

CONTENTS

7

So what meeting starter have you used lately that snared your group's attention or launched furious discussion?

Are your kids still talking about that opener—the one with the live cat, a bag, and a seventh-grade volunteer? Youth Specialties pays $25 (and in some cases, more) for unpublished, field-tested ideas that have worked for you.

You've probably been in youth work long enough to realize that sanitary, theoretical, tidy ideas aren't what in-the-trenches youth workers are looking for. They want—*you* want—imagination and take-'em-by-surprise novelty in meetings, parties, and other events. Ideas that have been tested and tempered and improved in the very real, very adolescent world you work in.

So here's what to do:

- Sit down at your computer, get your killer discussion or lesson starter out of your head and onto your hard drive, then e-mail it to ideas@youthspecialties.com. Or print it off and fax it to 619-440-4939 (Attn: Ideas).

- If you need to include diagrams, photos, art, or samples that help explain your idea, stick it all in an envelope and mail it to our street address: Ideas, 1224 Greenfield Dr., El Cajon, CA 92021-3399.

- Be sure to include your name and all your addresses and numbers.

- Let us have about three months to give your idea a thumbs up or down*, and a little longer for your 25 bucks.

*Hey, no offense intended if your idea isn't accepted. It's just that our fussy Ideas Library editor has these *really* meticulous standards. If the discussion or lesson starter isn't creative, original, and just plain fun in an utterly wild or delightful way, she'll reject it (reluctantly, though, because she has a tender heart). Sorry. But we figure you deserve only the best ideas.

ALPHABETICAL LIST
OF EVERY IDEA IN THIS BOOK

A Primer on Leading Discussions

A PRIMER ON LEADING DISCUSSIONS

Starting a discussion, and keeping it going...
the importance of confidentiality...asking questions that get responses...
and working with different personalities.

STARTING A DISCUSSION—
AND KEEPING IT GOING

Consider these 10 tips for creating a comfortable small-group atmosphere—a necessary quality if you want all students to enjoy participating.

1. Encourage your students to verbalize their views and feelings, however unorthodox they may be.

Nothing stifles a discussion faster than when kids don't feel safe to say what they feel. Small groups should be a place where adolescents can be honest about what they're thinking and feeling—no matter what's on their minds. What students discover for themselves remains with them far longer than anything you tell them. Be slow to correct them, but instead let them think through their own responses. This is usually a better way for them to make genuine and lasting discoveries about God.

2. Be grateful for every answer.

Yes, *every* answer. Leaders can also stifle

discussion by inadvertently making students feel silly or dumb about their responses and comments. Your job is to create a safe place for kids to say whatever they want—and be appreciated for it. Sure, if you work with seventh-grade males, you'll need to redirect gently the tangents that pop up every three minutes. (Hmmm...seventh grade males...did we say *gently*?) But it's generally better to encourage freedom of speech. Your kids will trust you (and themselves) more.

3. Don't be satisfied with the first response to your question.

Avoid setting a question-answer-question-answer pattern. Here's a better way to start a discussion. Ask for several responses to your question, then provoke the speakers to dialogue with each other. That is, move them from merely answering toward discussing or conversing—with each other, not just with you. Start the ball rolling in this direction by asking "Why do you think that?" and "What do the rest of you think?"

15

4. Keep the discussion moving.

A Bible study that does not move along at a good pace tends to get dull. Notice when kids are starting to lose interest, then quickly move on to the next question. If you must choose your evils, choose frustrated students who wanted to spend more time resolving an issue—not bored students who have been gradually distancing themselves from the 30-minute discussion between you and one other student. Jesus, you remember, often left questions unanswered. It helps people think for themselves.

5. Be alert to the individuals in your group.

Be aware of what's going on with your kids as they come to your small group. In fact, you may want to reserve the first few minutes of your small group for small talk and sharing. During your Bible study, notice when a student begins speaking, but stops. Look beyond those who are monopolizing the discussion, and deliberately ask other, quieter students for their responses. You'll never stop some personalities from standing out in your group; others will insist on staying in the background. That's okay. Your goal is to make every student feel that he or she is an important member of your group, whether or not each one contributes a lot to the discussion.

6. Don't be afraid of silence.

If your question gets no immediate response from a student, don't feel you have to jump in and answer it yourself. Let the question linger in the air for a while. And let kids know this, too. In fact, silence is often an answer in itself—or can be a necessary prelude to a deeply felt response. Of course, if every question you ask is met with prolonged silence, you may need to take a hard look at the kinds of questions you're asking. (More on asking good questions in "Ask Questions That Get Responses" on page 17.)

7. Turn difficult questions back to the group.

If you're intimidated by a student with a tough question, join the crowd. Yet that very question, tough as it may be, can be give you a chance to get a lively discussion going. Don't think you have to try to answer it—try turning the question

back to the group instead: "Whoa, good question. What do the rest of you think?" You may get some wild answers, but the students will be encouraged to think for themselves rather than look to you for answers. If a question remains unresolved, now and then challenge your small group to find the answer by your next meeting. (A prize can add some motivation here.)

8. Let your group self-correct its tangents.

The technique of turning a question back to the group is also a remedy for wild tangents. Don't just tell the student that he or she is wrong— ask instead, "What do the rest of you think?" Chances are as students give their input, the group will correct itself. This also encourages your students to dialogue with each other instead of directing their dialogue toward you.

9. Stay flexible to the group's needs.

Sooner or later (usually sooner), a student will come to her small-group meeting with a specific, significant, and often immediate concern that needs to be addressed in the context of the small group. It may be an unresolved conflict between group members, a friend (perhaps there that night) who wants to know more about Christ, a recent death, an impending divorce. Now is the time to put aside your agenda and deal with the issue. This shouldn't happen every week, however. Leading a small group requires the judgment to decide when an issue is sufficiently critical that you need to deal with it instead of leading your planned discussion.

10. Be prepared to learn from your group.

This is sometimes the best part of leading a small group. Your weekly preparation as well as the students' feedback can profoundly influence your own spiritual development. Ministry breeds maturity, and your ministry as a small-group leader will nurture your spiritual life as well as the spiritual lives of your students.

THE IMPORTANCE OF CONFIDENTIALITY

If you want kids to feel safe enough to share themselves deeply with others in their small group, then it's up to you to establish trust and confidentiality. Some small-group leaders use a written or verbal agreement, committing signers to the principle that whatever is shared in the group stays in the group. They don't tell their parents or their boyfriends the particulars of what they hear in their small group, and you don't tell your spouse.

If what you hear from a student during a meeting of your small group makes you think that a one-to-one talk would be appreciated or helpful, it is no breach of confidence for you to meet with the student over a hamburger later that week and talk personally.

There are critical exceptions to this rule, of course. If a student confides anything that even hints at physical or sexual abuse, you are *required* by some state laws to report that information to law-enforcement authorities. Know ahead of time what course of action is required of you by your supervisor, your church, and your state if you hear inklings of self-destructive or addictive behavior from students in your small group. At least you will probably talk to such students privately, recommending professional help with specific names and numbers. Keep an up-to-date list of local referral agencies for this purpose.

If confidence is broken in your group, deal with it immediately so that trust can be re-established. Meet privately with the group members who were involved, either individually or together, depending on circumstances. Your goal is to help kids learn when to share personal information with a third party, and when to keep such information to oneself.

ASK QUESTIONS THAT GET RESPONSES

Whether they're personal questions, topical questions, or Bible study questions, the way you ask them can make the difference between lively small-group discussions and dead ones.

Avoid yes or no questions.

Stay away from questions that begin with "Is there...?" "Are they...?" or "Do you think...?" Instead ask more *why* questions. For starters, run your questions by a friend before your small-group meeting and see if they're dead-end yes-or-no ques-

tions, or if they provoke exploration, opinions, and discussion.

Don't ask questions that assume an answer.

Asking "How does Jesus show his anger in this passage?" assumes that Jesus is angry and there is a right answer you want your kids to discover. The problem with such questions is that they tell students too much without leaving students room to discover answers and insights themselves. A better question: "What is Jesus feeling in this passage? Why do you think he feels this way?" Get ready for a much more interesting discussion!

Write questions that are relevant to your kids.

Some good questions will spring to your mind during the meeting, but don't rely on those. Instead spend some thinking time before the meeting—about where your kids are, what their maturity level is, what in the study is particularly relevant to your students—and thoughtfully write out most of your questions. Doing a Bible study on David and Bathsheba (2 Samuel 11)? Don't ask "What effect do you think David's sin of adultery had on his life?"—it's not nearly as relevant to kids as "What could David have done to keep from giving in to his lust for Bathsheba?" Kids are more apt to talk if questions clearly reflect issues in their own lives—and what they learn from the ensuing discussions will be more valuable to their spiritual journey.

Learn how and when to ask direct questions.

Direct questions like "Sue, is Jesus the Lord of your life?" may lead to meaningful dialogue, but only with the right people at the right time. The *wrong* time to ask questions this direct and personal is probably the small group's first meeting. Try the less threatening "How does Jesus become the Lord of your life?" and open it up to the group in general instead of directing the question to an individual. As your small group grows in trust and openness with each other, you can gradually use more direct questions to challenge your kids personally.

Ask questions that deal with feelings as well as facts.

Your goal is to engage your students' hearts as well as their minds. It's usually safer to deal with issues objectively ("What sins in St. Paul's list are teenagers at your school particularly inclined to?") rather than personally ("What sins in St. Paul's list should you give up?"). Yet the longer your small group meets, the deeper and more personal your questions can become.

WORKING WITH DIFFERENT PERSONALITIES

You know what it's like watching the individual personalities in a small group emerge—even if the small group is a family. Your challenge as a small-group leader is to learn to work with the personalities in your small group and help all your students grow individually even as they learn to function as a group.

Here are six types of student personalities, most of which you'll meet in a typical small group of teenagers. The aim isn't to stereotype students, but to forewarn you of common traits and characteristics you'll encounter in your small group—and then to help you find ways to minister more effectively to them.

The Talker

This is the student in your small group who never stops talking, who always has a comment for everything. You're tempted to apply duct tape, but don't—there are more productive ways to handle this student. First, position the Talker next to you when you begin your group, which reduces eye contact with her when you ask a question—and, when she interrupts someone, lets you reach over and touch her arm (usually a silent but effective cue). If you have a whole group of Talkers, you may want to try the ground rule that stipulates that the small group must circulate an object—a stuffed animal, Nerf Ball, spit wad, whatever—and that a student must possess it before speaking. This will help Talkers wait their turn.

Chances are, the Talker has some natural leadership ability that you should encourage. So let her lead the small group now and then. This can help her appreciate what you endure as a leader, and she just may become more supportive when *you* lead.

If the problem persists, get some time alone with her and talk with her about giving others a

chance to answer the questions. Help her feel that she's on your team, and that the two of you need to work together to encourage the other students to respond.

The Thinker

This student is quieter (and usually shier) than the others, with a tendency to get drowned out by the louder personalities in your group. So bring him out more by positioning him across from you, to increase the chances of eye contact with you. You can also use the tried-and-true method of occasionally directing questions to specific students, thereby eliciting responses from the Thinker.

If the Thinker is particularly shy, spend one-on-one time with him to discover what he's interested in—and so you can create the kinds of questions that will bring him into the discussion. Use the positive reinforcement of affirming him on those occasions when he actually *does* respond publicly. And when he lapses back into silence, don't interpret that silence as something that needs to be fixed. Some kids just learn best by listening and watching—and there's a good chance he's one of them.

The Church Kid

This kid has already spent more hours in this church than you probably have. She's progressed from the church nursery to the high school room in the course of her 14 or 15 years there. She consequently knows more about the Bible than any other kid in youth group, not to mention her small group. Of course, her knowledge may or may not indicate spiritual depth.

Church Kids can be the hardest to reach because they've heard it all, and therefore feel they have nothing to learn. One way to challenge them is by not being satisfied with pat answers. Always ask *why*. Or play devil's advocate by countering her squeaky-clean, correct answers with provocative arguments from the "wrong" side of the issue. Such strategies usually force a Church Kid to think more deeply about her answers instead of just rattling them off.

Ask her help you create questions for a Bible study—or even let her lead the small group once in a while. In any case, avoid asking questions that invite a "right" answer. Opt instead for questions that leave room for a variety of valid responses.

The Distracter

This is the student who can't sit still and ends up distracting everyone in your small group—including you. Rather than constantly stifling him, direct his energy toward productive ends: ask him to help you pass out Bibles, set up chairs, serve refreshments. Or (and this is good advice for all small groups, with or without Distracters) do some active-learning experiences with your small group—such as object lessons or field trips—instead of just sitting and talking week after week.

You may understand this student better (and where his energy comes from) if you get together with him outside of your small group. Even a Distracter can be good for your small group, if only because he doesn't let you get by with boring Bible studies. (Remember *that* when you're tempted to quit.) Really—your leadership skills will be sharpened as you find ways to engage him as well as the tranquil students in your lesson.

The Debater

She irritates you by challenging every point you (or anyone else) try to make. Sure, she brings a creative energy to the group sometimes—but she often stifles the other kids by making them feel too threatened to voice their opinions or feelings.

Deal with the Debater by establishing ground rules for your small group, the first (and perhaps the only) being: It's okay to disagree with opinions, but it is inappropriate to attack or put down other small-group members if their opinions differ from yours. A second ground rule may be that only one person may talk at a time. Ground rules like these help make a Debater's criticism less caustic and restrains her from interrupting others in order to make her point.

The good news: once Debaters understand and abide by such rules, their input can actually enliven your discussion. Just remember that your goal is to direct, not stifle, their participation.

The Crisis Producer

This student is in perpetual crisis—and lets your small group know about it every meeting. He's often self-absorbed and therefore unable to participate in the discussion, except when it's focused on him. So get together with him before your small group begins in order to talk through his problems with just you instead of bringing them to the small group. (Lucky you.) Or begin your small-group discussion with the assurance that everyone will have a chance to share problems, prayer requests, etc., at the end of the group. This helps members—and especially Crisis Producers—stay focused on your Bible study.

Whatever your strategy with your Crisis Producer, your goal is to help him see past his crises to some solutions. Then he will be able to participate in your small group without constantly having to bring the focus back to himself.

What about a student who raises a legitimate crisis during the discussion? Be flexible enough to postpone your study and deal with the issue at hand.

Adapted from The Youth Worker's Pocket Guide to Leading a Small Group *by Laurie Polich. Copyright 1997 by Youth Specialties.*

35 CREATIVE WAYS

TO START A DISCUSSION OR LESSON ON ANY TOPIC

**Here are techniques general enough to fit
just about any subject, but still quirky enough
to attract adolescent attention.**

GROUPERS

Groupers are unfinished sentences like "I wish I were..." They can be used to stimulate discussion. Through them, young people can express and explore their beliefs and goals. As a result, kids can discover what their values really are.

One way to use groupers is to follow these steps:

1. Give each participant a pencil and index card.

2. You can read aloud the groupers, write them on the board, or distribute them on index cards. Then have each person complete the groupers.

3. Encourage kids to complete their groupers honestly. No one will be graded or judged right or wrong. Every answer is acceptable. Each person has the right to decline to participate and the right to anonymity.

4. Collect the completed cards, read them aloud, and discuss them.

5. Conclude your discussion by reading your own grouper, and ask for feedback. Or read your grouper with the others so that kids won't know it's yours. Conclude with your own comments about the discussion.

Instead of reading answers for them, have kids read their own responses aloud. This works best if kids know each other well and if there is an atmosphere of freedom and trust among them. Kids can elaborate on their responses and answer group questions or not. All answers are acceptable, and kids can decline to participate.

Here is a sampling of groupers:

I fear most...
I wish I were...
I wish I were not...
I wish I had...
I wish I had not...
I wish I could...
If I were the leader of this country, I would...
The leader of this country should...
The happiest day of my life was...
If I could start this year over, I would...
My favorite place is...

My parents should...
I wish my parents wouldn't...
What hurts me the most is...
If I had $25, I would...
I would like to tell my best friend...
The worst thing a person could do is...
What always makes me mad is...
If I could do anything without being found out, I would...
I always cry when...
I always laugh when...
I hate...
If I were the principal of my school, I would...
If I had a million dollars, I would...
If my parents left me alone, I would...
The most important thing in my life is...
If I had X-ray vision, I would...
The hardest thing for me to do is...

NO-RISK DISCUSSION

Many young people are intimidated in church situations when asked to express opinions on controversial issues in front of their peers and/or adult leaders. This approach will allow them to say what they feel without fear of what others might think. Cut up paper strips, about 1½ inches by 8 inches. Give everyone a pencil and a strip of paper. Ask questions that require only short answers and ask them one at a time. Each student writes a number 1 at the top and answers the first question, then folds the paper down to conceal his or her answer. The papers are then passed to the person on the left and question number 2 is answered just below the folded-down portion. With each question, the paper is folded and passed to a new person until all the questions are answered. Collect the papers and redistribute them again and have everyone unfold the paper they received. As you repeat the questions for discussion, each person answers the way their paper reads. Usually the result will lead to further, less inhibited discussion, especially when students discover that their views are probably shared by quite a few others in the group. *Whitey White*

TAPE TALK

One of the best ways to get discussion going in a youth group is to bring in various points of view on a subject. One way to do this is by interviewing people outside of the youth group on tape or video and playing it for your youth group. For example, if the subject is love, interview a young child, an elderly person, and someone from an urban neighborhood, asking them how they would define love. Edit out the bad or dull ones and this can make an interesting program and a good discussion starter.

TEXTIMONY SERVICE

Do you have trouble getting your young people to share their experiences? Try a Textimony Service. On slips of paper write verses of Scripture dealing with some specific promises that the Lord makes to believers for their everyday lives. Then pass out the slips to the group and have them share how the Lord has been keeping that promise in their lives. If you like, you could let them pick their own verse to illustrate something that has been happening in their lives. Perhaps someone hasn't taken full advantage of a promise to which he is entitled; he might share that with the group. Someone else may have a helpful insight for that person. The group could pray for individual needs and needs that the whole group may have. Possible promises can be found in the following verses: Galations 5:18, Ephesians 2:14, John 16:23, John 14:27, John 10:10, Psalm 91:15 *(Reprinted with permission from HISWAY, 1445 Boonville, Springfield, Missouri, 65802)*

YARN-SHARING EXPERIENCE

In order to get your group members to open up and share their inner feelings and Christian experience, try using this technique. Take a ball of yarn (size is determined by the size of the group involved) and explain that you are going to ask them to participate in a little experiment. Tell them that in a moment you are going to throw the ball of yarn (while holding onto the end so the yarn will unwind) to someone in the group. The group should be standing in a circle. When that person catches the ball of yarn, she should share one of the following:
• What God has done for her
• What God has done for someone she knows
• What God has done for all of us (Christ's death, given us his Word, etc.)
• Something that she is thankful for

Then after she has shared one of the above, she will throw the ball to someone else in the circle (while holding onto the yarn) and the next person who catches the ball will also share one of the four things above. Keep this going until everyone in the group has had a chance to share at least once (several times is best, but this depends on the size of your group and the time you have).

After you have made a spider web pattern with the yarn and everyone has had a chance to share, stop the ball and begin to ask some questions:

1. What is this yarn doing for us physically? Answers would revolve around the idea of holding us together. (Before this you could comment that the effect of the sharing has created a somewhat beautiful web between the members of the group.) You could mention that for a beautiful pattern to evolve, everybody had to participate.

2. Have one or two members of the group drop their hold of the yarn. Immediately the center web becomes loose and the effect is for the circle to widen a little. Then ask: "What happens to the group when someone drops the yarn?" It becomes less close—looser knit and it makes something beautiful fall apart and turn ugly. You then could follow up with a brief talk on how the Bible teaches us to bear each other's problems, to share our happiness and sorrows, to be thankful, etc. You could emphasize that in sharing, a beautiful network of relationships and ties is formed, as is physically illustrated by the yarn, but it takes everyone to hold it together.

Jim Munson

MYSTERY GIFTS

Wrap several mystery gifts, using seasonal paper for wrapping. Vary the size of the boxes. Have several kids come up and select a gift from a box or pile of gifts. They open them (before the audience) then give an impromptu parable, thought, lesson, or something with the gift as a theme. If the treasury is able, the participants may keep the gifts. This is a great way to enhance creativity. *W.C. Arnold*

MYSTERY GUEST

Divide the youths into small groups of three or four per group. Then have each group choose a Bible character and research and collect information about him or her for 10 minutes. Each group gets a turn to take the stand, and the rest of the youths ask questions of the group to try to discover who the character is. Each question must be answered "yes," "don't know," or "no." If 10 "no" answers are given before the identity of the Bible character is guessed, the group wins. *James Brown*

RELAY DISCUSSION

Set up two, three, or four chairs (no more) in front of your group. Select a person to sit in each chair and explain that you are going to have a relay discussion. You, as the leader, will read out agree-disagree statements that beg debate or discussion. Only the people in the chairs up front can speak; everyone else listens. Once the statement has been read, the leader can turn the discussion over to those people or he can stimulate and encourage by asking their opinions. If a person in the front chairs does not want to speak about an issue, she may go out into the audience and tap anyone on the shoulder to take her place. The chosen person then must go up front and join in the discussion. Also, if any person in the audience has something to say at any time, he may run up front and replace any person there. Only the people in the front chairs can speak. Once you see the discussion slowing down, throw out a new statement. Also, to stimulate give and take, people can be assigned one point of view or the other, or certain chairs can be labeled AGREE and DISAGREE. Here are some sample discussion statements:

- Jesus identified more with the lifestyle of the poor than the rich; therefore, poor people make better Christians.
- The reason a church runs a youth program is to prove to itself that it is doing something for young people.
- A Christian should obey his government even if it violates the authority of Scripture.
- Abortion should be a decision left to the parents or parent of the fetus.
- Bad language is cultural and is thus not un-Christian.
- Physical violence can be justified by a Christian if it is in self-defense.
- It is wrong for a Christian to drink an alcoholic beverage.

• Christianity is the only religion through which a person can get to heaven.
• Our parents discipline us because they are trying to do what is best for us. *Dick Davis*

SPOTLIGHT MEETING

In a darkened room have kids sitting in a large circle. One person—usually the youth director or sponsor—has a spotlight (flashlight) that he shines on someone's face. Only the person the light is shining on may speak. The first round is usually word association or some nonthreatening kind of game just to get kids loosened up and into the spirit of things. In the second round, the person with the spotlight can ask each person he shines the light on one question, which they are to answer as honestly as possible. The spotlight draws everyone's attention to that one person and can be a very effective way for kids to share with each other. Questions can be as deep or shallow as the leader feels he wants to go without embarrassing anyone, but the questions should be designed to allow kids to honestly express themselves and their faith without fear. Allow anyone to pass if he is unable to answer the question. *Jim Hudson*

WISHING WELL

With the youth group seated in a circle, give each person two or three pennies. In the center, place a tub of water, which becomes your wishing well. Various puns can then be employed, such as "You can put in your two cents worth" or "A penny for your thoughts." Any person in the group who wants to speak—sharing some concern, a wish, something they are thankful for, a special blessing—throws a penny into the well and speaks. Make your well small enough so that it will take a little aim to sink the penny. This adds a little comic relief when some kids miss. Most kids will enjoy the experience and improvise as they go along, sharing pennies, pretending to throw a penny and making a "ker-plunk" sound, throwing nickels for "longer thoughts," and so on. Pennies can be saved and used again or given away. *Gregg Selander*

CURING DISCUSSION DOMINATORS

You know the pattern—a couple of kids dominate your discussions, while the rest sit and listen to what degenerates into a conversation between two or three people. Here's a fun and nonthreatening way to break the pattern.

Before beginning your next discussion, hand out two 3x5 cards to each group member. Establish these ground rules:
• Each time students (or sponsors!) want to make a comment, they must give one of their cards to the moderator of the discussion. Use your judgment to permit clarifying questions without losing a card.
• After both their cards are gone, students may make no more comments until all participants have used both their cards.

This method has two benefits: the normally talkative kids will do more thinking before they speak, weighing if the comments hanging on their tongues are worth using up a card. And because the normally quieter kids know that they must inevitably venture a comment sometime, they become more mentally involved—and usually make excellent contributions to the discussion. *David Wright*

HUMAN CONTINUUM

When discussing subjects that have many points of view, have the kids arrange themselves (prior to the discussion) in a human continuum from one extreme viewpoint to the opposite extreme. For example, if you are discussing drinking, have the kids line up with all those who are for drinking on one end and those who are against it at the other. Undecideds or moderates would be somewhere in the middle.

FOR	AGAINST

Kids may discuss the issue among themselves as they attempt to find the right spot in the line in relationship to each other. After they are settled, further discussion or debate can take place as kids attempt to defend their positions. Anyone may change positions at anytime. *Mike Renquist*

LEGOS GAME

The following experiment can be used with either adult youth sponsors or with kids. When used with sponsors it can demonstrate to them the advantages of allowing kids to discover truth on their own. With kids it will help them to see the value in using their heads rather than being fed the information.

First, divide your group into small groups of four or five. Then give each group a box of Legos with instructions to make something that works. Insist that each person has a say in the project. Kids will have a good time with this, so allow plenty of time. When the masterpieces are completed, ask each group to explain what they have.

Second, line everyone up in a single line. Scatter the Legos evenly throughout the line. Now you are the director and you guide them piece by piece to build a simple structure with the Legos. (For example: "Take the red pieces and fit them together like this.") It doesn't matter what you make but keep it simple. Don't let anyone get ahead of the group. If someone puts the piece in before you give the instruction, remove that person. Make everyone go step by step as you instruct them. When you finish go around the line and have the students tell you what they have. You will get different answers, but inform them that they can't tell you what they have because you are the one who made it and only you know what it is.

Third, it's time for discussion. Be sensitive to your own kids and their special needs as you discuss. The two experiments represent two ways of teaching. The first experiment guides the student to come up with something on his own that works. It is his and he has ownership of it. The second represents cramming your beliefs, prejudices, or opinions down the throat of the student. Ask which way they preferred, and have them give reasons. *Larry Jansen*

STRAW PICTURES

For this activity you will need boxes and boxes of ordinary drinking straws. You might try getting some donated by a local fast-food restaurant or a grocery store. Divide the kids into small groups and give each group a couple boxes of straws and a large place (maybe a 15-foot square) on the floor to work.

The leader then gives each group a topic or theme to be illustrated, using only the straws. The kids lay them around, placing them in position so that they eventually become a picture. The straws can be cut or hooked together, but that's all. Set a time limit and when all are finished, have some impartial judges award prizes for the best, most unusual, worst, and so forth. Topics can be just for laughs, or they can be more serious. At Christmas, for example, the group might put together a giant nativity scene, using straws. When it's completed, take some photos. *Marian Trievel*

STUDY BUBBLE

Find two large sheets of plastic, tape them together, add a fan (an ordinary household fan will suffice),

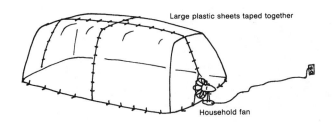

Large plastic sheets taped together

Household fan

and you've created a great new discussion place. It really works well, kids like it, and you can decorate it. *Geoffrey Koglin*

TRUTH OR DARE

Pass out two 3x5 cards and a pencil to each participant. On one set of cards students put questions about the Christian life—one per card—that they would like answered, fold them in half, and mark them with the letter T. These cards are placed in a box marked TRUTH. On the other set of cards they put Christian dares—one thing they dare another student to do for Christ during the next week (dares should be specific and possible). These cards are folded in half, marked with the letter D, and put in the DARE box.

Now, each participant chooses one card at random from the Truth box, answers the question, and tells why she thinks her answer is correct. No one else can speak until the person has answered. Then others can discuss whether they agree or disagree and why.

After the discussion, the participant draws a card from the Dare box, reads it to the group, and keeps the card to remind her to do the dare for Christ that week. Proceed until each person has answered a Truth question and chosen a Dare card. You can usually handle between six and nine questions in an hour, depending on how much discussion is allowed. For larger groups, divide into small groups of five or six.

Truth or Dare has been used successfully with high school youth. It lets you know what the kids are thinking, it gives them a chance to ask questions anonymously, and it challenges them to do something positive that week.

• **Dare Box.** You may want to challenge your kids to find creative ways to put their faith into action with the dares on page 29. Put each dare in a numbered envelope and seal it if you want to add a surprise element.

Then students read their dares, but they must keep them secret from the rest of the group until they've completed them. When a dare is completed, students can tell the rest of the group about the experience. If a dare is too intimidating to a student, allow that student to trade for a different one.

Larry Johnson and Leslie Riley

TALK IT OVER

This is a great discussion starter that provides a good exchange of ideas on a number of topics. Divide into groups of three. Give each group a list of statements such as the ones below and give each person a stack of 10 cards. Have the students number the cards one through 10. Students will choose one of the cards to represent their position on a scale of one through 10 as they discuss topics.

To begin, one person in each group reads a statement from the list. Students decide how strongly they agree or disagree with the statement and each chooses a number that reflects her position. A 10 indicates total agreement; a one indicates total disagreement. When everyone has chosen a card, students reveal them all at once.

If the numbers shown are all within a range of two, the group members don't need to discuss the issue—although they can if they want to. If the numbers are further apart than two, they must talk over the issue.

After 30 minutes, have the entire group come back together and share which statements generated the most discussion and which ones had the widest difference of opinion.

A variation is to have the kids use their fingers instead of using cards. For each statement, they would simply show the appropriate number of fingers. Some sample statements:

• I would leave a party shortly after arriving if I were not having a good time.
• I would discuss my personal family problems with friends.
• There are some crimes for which the death penalty should apply.
• If I were offered a less satisfying job at 25 percent increase in salary, I would take it.
• Parents should stay home from a long-awaited party to attend a sick child.
• I could forgive and forget if my mate were unfaithful.
• I think laundry is women's work.
• I think any teenager who wants birth control should be allowed to get it with no hassle.
• I would ask a friend to stop smoking around me if the smoke bothered me.
• A parent should immediately defend a child if the other parent is punishing the child unfairly.
• There should be no secrets between good friends.
• Housework done by the female is usually taken for granted by the male.
• I think there should be sex education in schools starting in kindergarten.
• I think there should be sex education in churches.
• Children should be spanked for some types of misbehavior.
• If a man enjoys housework and a woman enjoys a career, they should pursue these roles.
• It is a parent's duty to attend school functions in which their child is participating.
• I think it is important to remember birthdays of family and friends.
• I think it's okay for a 13-year-old to see an R-rated movie.
• Women with small children should not work unless it's a financial necessity.
• Marijuana should be legalized.
• Kids should not have to account for an allowance.
• Parents should regulate how much TV a small child can watch.
• Schools should eliminate the use of grades.
• I would say something if I saw a friend littering.

Syd Schnaars

DARE BOX

Ask for a salvation testimony from one of the elders of our church. Be prepared to share parts of it with the class.

Read Philippians chapter 1. Write a letter to your parents expressing your thankfulness for their support in your life.

Memorize the first chapter of James. Recite it for the class.

Select a secret pal from the youth group and do something special for that person every day for one week.

Ask for a missions testimony from someone on the missions committee. Share it with the class.

Offer to work in the nursery next Sunday in someone's place.

Bake a batch of brownies or cookies for one of the leaders in our church, with a note that simply says, "Thanks!"

Wash your parents' car. Accept no money for doing it.

Empty all the trash cans in your house and scrub them all with soap and water.

Make a phone call to someone who is not in Sunday school this week but should be.

Send a funny card to someone who needs encouragement.

Give one of your parents a back rub.

Choose a favorite Scripture passage and share it with the class. What does it mean to you?

Ask our pianist the following questions: When did you join our church? What was your most moving experience at our church? What do you think have been the three greatest events in the history of this church? What is the funniest thing that ever happened in our church? When you were my age, what was your Sunday school group like?

Ask the chairman of the deacon board the following questions: When did you join our church? What was your most moving experience at our church? What do you think have been the three greatest events in the history of this church? What is the funniest thing that ever happened in our church? When you were my age, what was your Sunday school group like?

Ask the oldest member of our church the following questions: When did you join our church? What was your most moving experience at our church? What do you think have been the three greatest events in the history of this church? What is the funniest thing that ever happened in our church? When you were my age, what was your Sunday school group like?

Watch a movie and answer the following questions: Who do you think is the hero of this movie? Who is the villain? Why? What is the bad or evil thing that could or does happen? How is the evil dealt with? What do you think the producer and director are trying to teach us through this movie? Do you agree with what they are saying? Do you feel this movie will help build up your relationship to God, your family, or your friends? Read Philippians 4:8-9.

Watch a music video and answer the following questions: Name the music video and the artist. Did you like this video? Why or why not? Did the visuals have anything to do with the song? What was the song about? What did the person singing the song want to happen? Is this a good thing? Why? Do you think that this is a video a Christian could recommend as good for someone to watch or listen to? Why? Does it fit the qualifications that Paul wrote about in Philippians 4:8-9? How?

PHOBIA MONTH

Here's an idea you do not need to be afraid of. Plan a phobia month during which you have lessons in areas your kids are finding difficult. To build interest keep the subject matter of each session a secret except for the name of the related phobia. For example, advertise a discussion on Christmas season depression as Santa Claustrophobia Night.

Here are some other possibilities:

Fear of—	Condition Name—
aloneness	monophobia
crowds	ochlophobia
darkness	nyctophobia
death	thanataphobia
The Devil	demonophobia
failure	kakorrhaphiophobia
God	theophobia
hell	hadephobia
jealousy	zelophobia
being looked at	scopophobia
marriage	gamophobia
pain	algophobia
poverty	peniaphobia
responsibility	hypengyophobia
ridicule	categelophobia
school	schoolphobia
sin	hamartophobia
work	ponophobia

Your kids probably won't have any of these phobias, but they are topics that sometimes can cause fear and concern. This will give you a different approach to some important topics for your youths. *Aaron Bell*

HANGMAN LESSONS

If you have a good idea for a lesson but aren't sure how to present it, play Hangman to reveal your outline. For example, four points on a lesson about friendship might be Acquaintance, Casual, Special, and Intimate. Instead of just telling your group these points, have kids guess each word a letter at a time. For every wrong guess, hang a part of the body from the noose. Teens will usually guess the word and will become more involved in the lesson.

John Stumbo

LIGHTS ON, LIGHTS OFF

This idea can be used as a discussion starter with any topic, or it can be used simply as a fun way to test everyone's power of concentration. You will need some large drawings, photographs, or slides.

Give each person a sheet of paper. Have kids number down the left side of their sheets corresponding to the number of pictures you will show. Have them create three columns across the top of the page (Columns A, B, and C). They should write their answers in each column as they view each picture. Here are the three questions they should answer for each picture:

1. What is the first word that this picture brings to your mind?
2. What feeling did you experience when the picture was revealed?
3. Write a sentence that summarizes the picture.

Turn out the lights and put up the first picture. Flip the lights on for five or 10 seconds and then off

	1. What is the first word that this picture brings to your mind?	2. What feeling did you experience when the picture was revealed?	3. Write a sentence that summarizes the picture.
1 2 3 4 5 6 7 8 9 10			

again. (If you are using slides, simply show the slide for a few seconds while the lights are off.) Next, remove the picture and put the lights back on just long enough for the kids to write down their responses. Repeat this for each picture.

After viewing all of the pictures, discuss your group's responses, pointing out the differences and the various points of view that arise concerning the pictures. The goal is to help the group learn to appreciate other viewpoints. *John Peters*

WORD PICTURES

Here's an idea that can help your teens do word studies, examine Bible characters, or delve into theological concepts. Pass out worksheets (page 32) with a word picture diagram printed on them. Have your group members write the key word (it can be any word or name you suggest) in the center.

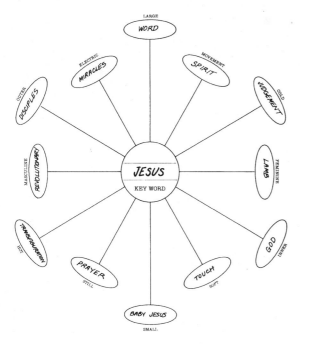

Then, combining the key word with the guide words on the outside, ask them to write in additional descriptive words. See our sample. It's easiest to write the first thing that comes to mind. When teens have completed this exercise, they will have a better understanding of the key word and will be able to see more of the implications involved in study of Scripture. *Keith Curran*

CRISIS RESPONSE

This is a good activity to help your kids develop their abilities to deal with difficult situations quickly and decisively. It stimulates thinking, and it encourages kids to realize that they really can come up with answers to tough issues on their own. Divide into small groups of three or four. Select a panel of judges (adult sponsors or a group of kids). Next, present a problem, crisis, or ministry situation to the entire group. Here's an example:

> You are at school one day, getting something out of your locker, and you accidentally slam your finger in the locker door. Under your breath, you let out a choice swear word. A friend overhears this and says to you, "Hey, I thought

Christians didn't say things like that." Now what do you say?

Give the groups exactly one minute to come up with a response to the situation. Each group has one person (a different person each time) present the group's response.

After this, the panel of judges chooses the best response and explains why. It's a good idea for the judges to affirm the groups whose ideas are not chosen as well.

This approach adds the elements of fun and competition to learning in a very effective way.
Alan Hamilton

RUG DISCUSSION

Here's a great idea to use when you just don't have time to plan your usual terrific youth meeting. It's simple and works like a program that you've spent hours working on.

Pass out 3x5 cards to everyone in the room. If you have a topic you were planning to discuss, ask the kids to write out a question relating to the theme about something that's been bothering them or that they're struggling with in their lives. If you aren't using a theme, then they can just write out questions they have of any kind. Cards should not be signed.

You will get a great variety of questions. After kids finish writing them, pass a box or container around the room to collect them. Have the leader read the questions, one at a time, and let the kids suggest some answers.

This is a useful approach to questions because kids can often do a great deal to help out their peers and because honest questions can be asked when they're anonymous. To make this a "rug" discussion, have all the finished 3x5 cards thrown on the rug in the center of a discussion circle, mixed up, and then read. Kids love it.
Mark C. Christian

SPIRITUAL ADVENTURELAND

Many games can be used to teach spiritual truths. The following ideas will give you an idea of how you might follow up after games your kids enjoy. Many scriptural principles and applications can be

Word Picture

This is a worksheet for you to produce a word picture uniquely your own. You will be surprised at the new light you bring to the key word in the center of the picture. You may even be surprised at how creative you really are.

Directions: Write the key word in the center circle. Fill in the smaller circles using the nearby words as guides. You can write down words that are opposites to the guide words if you like. This is your picture of the key word. Have fun.

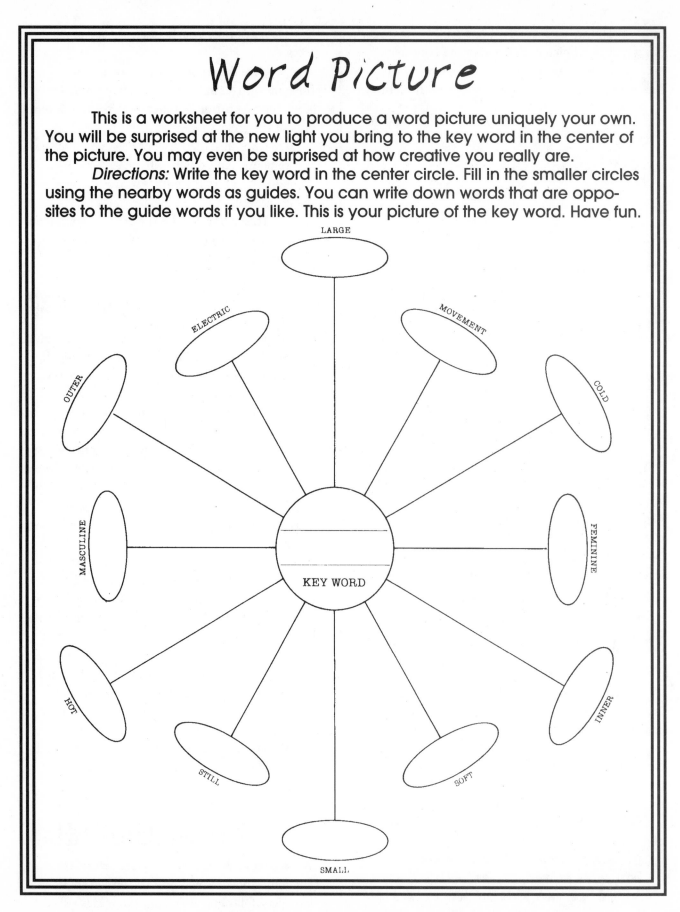

found in the simplest and wildest of games if you look for them. Such an approach is especially good for junior highers and kids who don't enjoy sitting in one place for very long.

• **Line Pull.** Two teams line up on opposite sides of a line and try to pull members of the other team across the line. Once a person is pulled across the line, he becomes a member of the opposing team. After playing by these rules for a while, put everyone on one side of the line except for one strong guy, who is the only one on his team.

Have someone read John 6:40-48. Ask the question "What does Jesus mean when he says, 'No one can come to me unless the Father who sent me draws him'?" Ask the kids to compare the game they just played with that statement.

• **Sardines.** This game is essentially hide-and-go-seek in reverse. One person—"It"—hides. As other players find "It," they hide with "It." Pretty soon more people are hiding than are looking. The object is to avoid being the last person to find the hidden group.

Ask someone to read Philippians 3:7-16. Divide the kids into groups of four and ask them to design a coat of arms that displays what Paul knew to be the purpose of life. This Scripture centers on Paul's desire to be like Christ and to share in his sufferings.

• **Hares and Hounds.** Have everyone stay in one room for a few minutes while two members of the group go through the church (or wherever you are playing), leaving a trail to another point in the church. The trail can be marked with small pieces of paper, by adjusting the furniture, or whatever. It should be clear, yet only traceable by careful, deliberate observation. The object of the game is to track successfully the two volunteers after they have completed the trail. The challenge is not to track them quickly but simply to track them successfully.

Have someone read Mark 1:16-20. Ask the kids, "What did it mean to those people to follow Christ? How did the game simulate what you go through as you try to follow Christ?" At this point, you can enter into a discussion of the lordship of Christ, and allow the kids to reflect on how they attempt to follow Christ in their daily lives.

Jim Walton

SITCOM DISCUSSIONS

To encourage discussion and creative thinking about any topic, divide into small groups of four or five people and assign each group a popular TV situation comedy and a topic. The task is to dramatize

the topic, using the characters and format of their particular sitcoms. If the topic is substance abuse, for example, the group would act out a typical scene from the program, playing the show's characters— but in the process communicating tips, warnings, or whatever, about substance abuse.

Choose from current sitcoms or old classics.

This activity is not only a lot of fun, but produces some great discussion as you debrief each performance. *Michael W. Capps*

TRIANGULAR TEACHING

Teaching can be enhanced considerably simply by how the room is set up. The following idea is a good set-up for teaching about the Trinity, the three

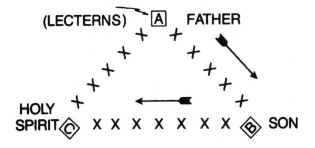

loves—agape, philos, and eros—or any other topic that has three or four distinct points.

Set up the chairs in a triangle, so that they face the middle. At each corner of the triangle, place a speaker's stand.

When you get to the part in your lesson about God the Father, for example, you stand in corner A. When you teach about God the Son, you move to corner B—and then finally on to corner C when you teach about God the Holy Spirit. During the discussion after the lesson, follow the same pattern: move from corner to corner, depending on which person of the Trinity you are discussing.

This sort of arrangement offers variety, as well as helping kids to keep things clear in their minds during the lesson. Use any variation of this that fits your facilities or your lesson. *Michael W. Capps*

FISH BOWL

Ease your teens into Scripture reading and sharing by playing Fish Bowl. Arrange chairs in a circle, with one chair in the middle.

PUTTING LOVE IN ACTION
(Matthew 5:7)

Love is not merely a nice feeling. God's love is action in the form of mercy. Before the Sermon on the Mount, Jesus had healed large numbers of suffering people; he had eaten supper with Matthew—a despised, rejected tax collector—as well as the undesirables at Matthew's place—people who had dubious morals, who used coarse language, who drank and ate to excess. His only comment to the Pharisees, who criticized his choice of company, was "Mercy—not sacrifice—is what pleases God."

Love is love only if it is put into action, only if it is given away, only if it looks and focuses on the good in others and their needs. It would have been easy for Jesus to dwell on the negative in others, but he always drew attention to the positive, good qualities that people possessed—even if they themselves were unaware of theirs. That is love in action—to be merciful as God is merciful. What are your thoughts?

Whoever sits in the middle is in the fish bowl and does the talking.

Next prepare some devotionals on note cards—a Scripture verse and a brief commentary, with perhaps a question that invites readers to add to the commentary or to share their thoughts.

Add the note card with the Scripture reading to a stack of blank cards, then deal out the cards at random to the kids. Whoever receives the card with the Scripture reading goes into the fish bowl, reads the Scripture and the commentary, and responds to the question. If a student gets the card more than twice, she has the option to choose someone else to take her place. *David Washburn*

ON THE SPOT

Even in a small group, it is not as easy to initiate honest dialogue between members on serious, risky topics in a safe, controlled atmosphere. If your group is small, On the Spot will give all participants the full attention of the group, without competition or interruption, as they attempt whatever degree of personal transparency they are comfortable with. The game adapts to your group's needs and is especially appropriate for late-night discussion starters at retreats.

Prepare three stacks of cards—a stack of low-risk questions, a stack of high-risk questions, and a stack of PASS cards. The three types of cards should be three different colors.

Sample low-risk questions:

• If Jesus visited my school this week, three things he'd want to change immediately are _____, _____, and _____.

• To be popular at my school, you must _____.
• I think most people spend too much time _____.
• Most people think Christians are too _____.
• Three facts that most people don't know about Jesus are _____, _____, and _____.

High-risk questions:

• If Jesus had been visibly with me today, I would not have said three things I did. They are _____, _____, and _____.

• The man, woman, or child in the Bible most like me is _____.

• I felt farthest from God when _____.
• Two details about myself I like most are _____ and _____.

• One thing that God most wants me to change is _____.

Here's how the game proceeds. Each player is given the same number of PASS cards—usually one or two, depending on how frank players feel like being with each other. One person is chosen to be on the spot. The next player to the right is the dealer, who in this game deals out questions, not cards.

Whoever is on the spot chooses which pile to answer a question from. The dealer takes the top card from that pile and reads it aloud. The on-the-spot player has 30 seconds to answer the question honestly. The dealer then has the option to ask the same player a question of his own. After this second question, the on-the-spot player can choose to either entertain more questions on that topic from anyone in the group or elect not to, in which case play moves clockwise and a new player is on the spot.

A typical round sounds like this:

DEALER: (selecting card from the stack that was chosen and reads) I think most people spend too much money on _____.

ON THE SPOT: Hmm. I think most people spend too much money on clothes.

DEALER: Do you think you spend too much money on clothes?

ON THE SPOT: Yes, I guess so. It's a big priority for me to look nice, but I don't think there's anything especially wrong with that.

PASS cards are played by at any time in order to escape an especially risky or embarrassing question. Play passes immediately clockwise when a PASS card is used. Encourage students to use their PASS cards rather than be less than completely honest. On the other hand, PASS cards must be used strategically—if a player uses them up too quickly, the player must answer the questions.

Control the flow of the game, and permit no interruptions or speaking out of turn. There are no wrong answers, no points are scored, and everyone wins. *Mary Gillett*

Video Intros

For a fun way to introduce a lesson, say, on God's love, is to get a video camera and tape the leader asking a question like "How do you know that God really loves you?" Then, as if in response to that question, videotape the answers of some of your kids to the slightly different question, "How do you know your boyfriend/girlfriend really loves you?" Their answers will play back immediately following the original question, making for hilarious results. Make sure the kids you videotape use only the pronoun he or she in their answers, and not proper names or other references. *Todd Hinkie*

How Do You Feel?

To help kids express their feelings to each other in creative ways, form small groups in which students express how they are feeling in terms of, say, automobiles: "I feel like a red Porsche" or "I'm just about out of gas right now."

Here are more subjects and images to choose from:

Car	Flower	Song	Number
Toy	Color	Year	Day
Month	Season	Stone	Fruit
Vegetable	Flavor	Holiday	Sandwich
Candy	Road sign	Recipes	Sewing
Book	Clothes	Shoes	Time
Money	Jewelry	Furniture	Animal
Building	Sport	Movie	Cookie
Cake	Beverage	Fabric	Cereal
Ice cream	Feeling word	Temperature	Weather

Sherry Wingert

Chutes and Ladders

Life is full of ups and downs. Using a Chutes and Ladders game board and rules, play with the following additions: When a player lands on a ladder, he describes a good experience; when landing on a chute, he describes a bad experience. If players have trouble thinking of specific experiences, use the following questions to prompt them:

- What was the experience?
- Has the experience left a lasting impression on you?
- Would you describe the lesson as a reward or a reprimand?
- How have you grown from this experience?

Conclude the play by discussing the kinds of experiences that individuals apparently have little control over—like the roll of the die. Ask the group how they think God fits into these kinds of experiences. Ask how God is a part of the good and the bad in our lives. *Laurie Delgatto*

KIDS ON CAMPUS

Here's a good way to identify different kinds of problems kids deal with. Bring in an assortment of common items to use as object lessons to generate discussion about the characters you describe.

• **Mr. Clean** represents church kids—those who think they have it all together. Though they look good on the outside, there can be a lot of struggles on the inside. How do we relate to kids like that?

• **Cover Girl make-up** represents kids who are preoccupied with their appearance. They want to look good, no matter what it costs. Why do you think some people are obsessed with their looks? What should our attitude be?
• **Beer cans** symbolize the party guys at school. Their idea of fun is getting wasted, getting in trouble, and acting like jerks. Is it possible that their behavior is a smoke screen for a lot of pain on the inside? How can we reach out to guys like this?
• **Chunky candy bar** illustrates overweight kids left out of certain circles or kids who may be loners for other reasons. Their isolation may be obvious, or they may hide it by laughing at themselves, pretending to be jolly and content. Any ideas about sharing Christ with kids like these?
• **Aspirin** portrays Johnny Advil—the kid who gives you a headache. He's obnoxious and seems to go out of his way to irritate

you. You wish he'd leave you alone. But what do you think Johnny's real problem is?
• **National Enquirer** represents the person who spreads rumors about everyone. He or she has a tongue of fire and loves to cut people down. How do you feel when people spread rumors about you? What can be done about it?

These are ideas to get you started—add others as you wish; the possibilities are endless. *Tim Freet*

NAME THAT SIN!

This game-show activity also makes an easy and entertaining opener for a weekly meeting—especially if your lesson is about one of the sins mentioned in this game.

The emcee (you or a sponsor) runs into the room and in typical Guy Smiley fashion shouts, "It's time to plaaaay...'Name That Sin,' the game where knowing your sins wins you big prizes!" The emcee then divides the group into two teams, or—if the group is large (50 or more)—selects a five-student panel from each team, and the rest of the students cheer for their representatives.

The game itself is simple. The emcee reads the question (see a sample list below; answers follow in parentheses), and the first player to raise a hand has a chance to answer. Remind players that they should respond with the predominant sin, not the related, subtle ones underlying the problem. If the answer is wrong, the other team gets a chance to answer the question—and so on, until there are three wrong answers, and then the question is thrown out. Award a point per correct answer—or three points if the answer is given on the first attempt, two points on the second attempt, and one point on the third attempt.

The emcee can toss a Tootsie Roll (or similar small treat) to players who give correct answers. All members of the winning team get a prize at the end of a round.

• **Your best friend gets a new car and you wish she'd die of a disease and leave the car to you. Name that sin!** *(covetousness or envy)*
• **Your girlfriend smiles at another guy, and you want to kill him. Name that sin!** *(jealousy)*
• **Your parents forbid you to see a movie, but your friends talk you**

into it and you go. Name that sin! *(disobedience)*

• During the prayer-and-share time in Sunday school, you mention your grandparents' $1000 gift and explain how you plan to spend it. Name that sin! *(boasting)*

• You replay the bedroom scene three times in a movie you rented. Name that sin! *(lust)*

• When your friend tells you in confidence that she might be pregnant, you tell a couple of your friends at church—just so they can pray about it. Name that sin! *(gossip)*

• You've just turned 21, you're out to dinner with some younger Christian friends, and to celebrate you order a beer with your meal. They wish they could have one. Name that sin! *(causing a weaker brother to stumble)*

• Your curfew is midnight. You get home at 12:20 a.m. In the morning your parents ask what time you got in, and you answer, "Around 12:00." Name that sin! *(lying)*

• You reject Jesus as Savior and Lord. Name that sin! *(unbelief)*

• Your sister borrows your best sweater without asking you and accidentally ruins it. She's miserable about it, apologizes to you, and even offers to replace the sweater. You don't speak to her. Name that sin! *(unforgiveness)*

• When you get a new car, you spend most nights and weekends either working on it or working at a job for cash to spend on the car. Name that sin! *(idol worship)*

• You figure that as long as you and your girlfriend don't go all the way, it doesn't really matter what else you do. Name that sin! *(sexual immorality)*

• You "accidentally" let a newspaper clipping about your recent football accomplishments fall out of your Bible during Sunday school in front of the girls so they will comment on your achievements. Name that sin! *(pride)*

• You tell your little sister never to touch your things—but when you're out of hair spray, you use hers without asking. Name that sin! *(hypocrisy)*

• You're mad at your little brother, so you purposely leave his hamster cage open so it can escape. Name that sin! *(malice)*

Or vary the game's title and questions to match your teaching series—"Name That Old Testament Prophet," "Name That Spiritual Gift," "Name That Prophecy," "Name That Parable," etc. *Lynne Marian*

THIS BOTHERS ME

Here's an idea that seeks to get kids to air their gripes or hang-ups about whatever topic you want to address. It can be set up like a TV game show entitled "This Bothers Me" or "What's Buggin' You?" The kids are the players and the youth leader is the host. The rules are simple: A kid tells what bothers him most about the topic, and the group members vote for the complaints they agree with the most. Each kid in the group gets a chance to describe what really bugs him or her the most. You can then use the answers the kids give as a springboard for discussion. *Phil Print*

STUMP THE SPEAKER

Here's a youth group version of Stump the Band, a game that's been featured on "The Tonight Show" for many years.

Ask kids to find objects in their pockets, purses, or around the room. Call on students one at a time to give you their objects. You then have 15 seconds to think up a 30-second object lesson, using that item to teach a spiritual truth. If you can't do it, but the student can, the student wins a prize.

This game will get your creative juices flowing—plus, it's a great way to pass the time if you finish your Sunday school lesson early and are waiting for dismissal. As a variation select kids to be the speaker. *Michael Frisbie*

DISCUSSION & LESSON STARTERS

BY TOPIC

What subject are you teaching this week? Look up your subject (they're arranged alphabetically, starting on this page). Then choose the opener that fits your discussion (or lesson) and—most importantly—your group. In fact, with the merest of tweaking, many of these openers are virtually complete lessons in themselves, with questions, activities, parables, object lessons—all designed to draw opinions, thoughts, and feelings from your students.

ADVERTISING ETHICS

AD VALUES

This exercise can really sensitize young people to be more aware of the advertisements to which they are exposed. Give the group a selection of magazines that have plenty of ads. Supply enough so that each person can have one. Also give each person a list of character traits, both positive and negative, such as the ones below, with room beside each trait to keep score. Ask the youths to go through their magazines and try to match the ads with the traits on their list. When they see an ad that appeals to a certain trait, then they make a mark beside that trait. Here is a sample list:

- Wealth, luxury, greed
- Security (no worries)
- Sexual or physical attractiveness
- Intelligence
- Conformity (join the crowd)
- Freedom (do what you want—no responsibility)
- Justice, human rights (concern for others)
- Power, strength
- Responsibility
- Ego, pride
- Status (being looked up to)
- Escapism
- Humility, self-sacrifice
- Self-control
- Ease, comfort

After everyone has finished, discuss the results. To what conclusions can you come about the kind of traits to which most advertisements appeal? Do they bring out the best or the worst in people? Do very many ads appeal to Christian values? *Tom Spilker*

COMMERCIAL CONFORMITY

When your group discusses the subtle worldliness that tends to creep into Christians' homes and thoughts and behavior (Romans 12:1-2, Matthew 6:19-33, and Colossians 3:1-2), bring with you a video of prime-time commercials that you taped. Replay them as you ponder questions like these:

- What's really being sold in this ad?
- What else besides the product itself is being promoted?
- Is there anything unusual or strange in the ad?
- What sells you on the product?
- Does this ad make girls or guys look stupid or used? (Beer commercials often excel at this.)
- How are you initially affected by the commercial?
- How do certain ads focus on guilt and feelings of inadequacy in us?
- Is your worth to society based on your beauty, youth, or possessions?
- How, if at all, is your value system affected?

Grant Sawatzky

GUESS THE JINGLE

Most teens insist that they don't pay attention to objectionable lyrics in the secular music they hear, and so those lyrics don't have any effect on them. To make the point that song lyrics do indeed work their way into the listeners' minds whether they realize it or not, try this game.

Have ready a list of 15 or more familiar commercial jingles you can hum or whistle. Then divide into teams by age, grade, school, or sex. Present each jingle tune, stopping when one team or the other is able to guess correctly the product that jingle is trying to sell. Every correct guess earns 100 points for the guesser's team; every incorrect guess loses the team 100 points. When you've exhausted your list, some of the kids might volunteer to do their own. The team with the highest score wins.

The game is fun in itself and will generate excitement, but the important part is the discussion that follows. Point out that most people don't consistently pay attention to the words of commercial jingles, yet the message gets through. In fact, American businesses spend billions of dollars each year to write and produce those jingles because they believe lyrics will influence our behavior. Finally, make the connection explicit: If jingles can affect our thinking, attitudes, and behavior, perhaps the contemporary music we listen to does the same, even if we don't consciously pay attention to the lyrics. *David C. Wright*

THE ULTIMATE KEN AND BARBIE

Form small groups of three to six kids, and give each group the following supplies: old magazines (*Sports Illustrated*, *Glamour*, *Vogue*, *Seventeen*), glue, scissors, and newsprint. Assign each group the task of creating from magazine cutouts the perfect Ken and Barbie. From different models they should cut out the best pair of legs, the greatest biceps, the most beautiful hair, the most alluring eyes—in short, they should create the ultimate body (which will appear deformed and add to the fun).

After gluing these parts to the newsprint, create the ultimate setting of beautiful home furnishings, exotic cars, electronic toys, landscape artistry—everything society says we need in order to be happy. Once the small groups have hung their contributions on the wall, let the whole group vote on the best collage. Conclude by helping the "artists" look at our society with God's perspective: he looks at the heart (1 Samuel 16:7). Besides, after he had made us—and before Sony, Guess, and Toyota had cluttered our lives—he said his creation was good. *Chuck Hawkins*

ATHEISM

STONE AN ATHEIST

This is a unique way to see how secure your kids are in the Christian walk. It will expose them to hidden attitudes they may have toward people who don't call themselves Christian. It will also show them their need to understand how to witness, and the importance of having a working knowledge of Scripture.

To begin, you must recruit someone who is a Christian to role-play an atheist. Whoever this person is, she must not be known by any of the kids. The person should be prepared to speak about 15 minutes on why she doesn't believe in God. Areas to be included in the speech could be:

- The problem of evil in the world
- Hypocrisy in the church

- How church history is filled with brutality and war in the name of God
- Evolution and other theories of science that contradict Scripture
- The church's seeming unconcern for the ills of society
- The existence of many different religions in a variety of cultures

You may even tell the kids that you have invited an atheist to speak on the subject of "Why I don't believe in God." Following the speaker's 15-minute speech, instruct her to have a discussion period, with questions from the kids. Now sit back and watch the stones be thrown! Be sure to take notes on the kids' reaction to this atheist. Don't talk or get involved yourself.

Stop the discussion after about 15 minutes and reveal the secret. Now you can lead a discussion with some of the following questions:

- What was your attitude toward the atheist when you couldn't answer her during the speech?
- Did you feel frustrated over not being able to give an adequate answer to all the problems she mentioned?
- Was there any truth in some of her complaints? If so, how did you feel about it?
- What should the church be doing in society to minister to society's ills?
- What about the problem of hypocrisy in the church?
- How can we in love minister to those around us who don't believe in God?

Dennis Marquardt

ATHEIST ROLE-PLAY

This is a simple discussion starter that deals with the question "Does God really exist?" Sometimes it's a good idea to force kids to think through their reasons for believing in God (if they say they do) and to strengthen those beliefs. In addition, it is important to take students a step further and help them see how their belief (or nonbelief) in God makes a difference in the way they live.

Begin with a role-play. Have the kids pair off. One person takes the role of an atheist (a person who does not believe in God) and the other is a believer. For about three minutes have the youth assume these roles and try to convince the other person that their view is the correct one. After they

have done this, have another person (such as one of the youth sponsors) come before the group and take the position of the atheist. The group must try to convince him that he is wrong. Since the students have had some practice in their individual role-plays, they should be well equipped to do so.

The next step is to give the kids pencil and paper, and to ask them to write down five things that would change in their lives if they knew there was no God. What difference would it make in the way they lived? Next, have them write down five things that would probably change in their lives if they knew for a fact that there really was a God. In other words, how would their lives be different from the way they are now if God somehow made himself known (by appearing in the sky, or something like that) so that there was absolutely no doubt whatsoever that he existed. How would they behave differently?

Now have the students compare their lists and discuss the differences between both lists and the way they live right now.

Follow this up with a discussion. Some possible questions:

- On the basis of arguments presented, do you believe in God or not? (You might have a vote, secret ballot if you want.)
- Is it possible to abstain in a vote for or against the existence of God? In other words, can a person just not have an opinion? What are the consequences of such a position?
- How does your belief affect the way you live right now?

Ken Potts

DEAR BELIEVER

A pamphlet published by the Freedom From Religion Foundation in Madison, Wisconsin, is reproduced in part on page 44.

Hand out copies to your group, then set the students off on a mission to answer the articulate and potent arguments in this pamphlet. Direct them to get answers to the objections in this pamphlet from wherever they want—the Bible, their parents, other adults in the church, wherever. Then have them use their research to write a response.

Dear Believer

You ask me to consider Christianity as the answer for my life. I have done that. I consider it untrue, repugnant, and harmful.

I find it incredible that you ask me to believe that the earth was created in six literal days; women come from a man's rib; a snake, a donkey, and a burning bush spoke human language; all animal species, millions of them, rode on one boat; a detached hand floated in the air and wrote on a wall; Jesus walked on water unaided; fish and bread magically multiplied to feed the hungry; water instantly turned into wine; a fiery lake of eternal torment awaits unbelievers under the earth while there is life after death in a city that is 1,500 miles cubed, with mansions and food, for Christians only.

If you believe these stories, then you are the one with the problem, not me. These myths violate natural law, contradict science, and fail to correspond to reality or logic. If you can't see that, then you can't separate truth from fantasy. It doesn't matter how many people accept the delusions inflicted by "holy" men; a widely held lie is still a lie.

If Christianity were simply untrue, I would not be too concerned. Santa is untrue, but it is a harmless myth that people outgrow. But Christianity, beside being false, is also abhorrent. It amazes me that you claim to love the God of the Bible, a hateful, arrogant, sexist, cruel being who can't tolerate criticism. I would not want to live in the same neighborhood as such a creature!

The biblical God is a macho male warrior. Though he said, "Thou shalt not kill," he ordered death for all opposition. He punished offspring to the fourth generation; ordered pregnant women and children to be ripped up; is partial to one race of people; judges women as inferior to men; is a sadist who created a hell to torture unbelievers; created evil; spread dung on people's faces; sent bears to devour 42 children who teased a prophet; punished people with snakes, dogs, dragons, swords, axes, fire, famine, and infanticide; and said fathers should eat their sons. Is that nice? Would you want to live next door to such a person?

And Jesus is a chip off the old block. He said, "I and my father are one," and he upheld "every jot and tittle" of the Old Testament law. He preached the same old judgment: vengeance and death, wrath and distress, hell and torture for all nonconformists. He never denounced the subjugation of slaves or women. He irrationally cursed and withered a fig tree for being barren out of season. He mandated burning unbelievers. (The Church has complied with relish.) He stole a horse. You want me to accept Jesus, but I think I'll pick my own friends, thank you.I also find Christianity to be morally repugnant. The concepts of original sin, depravity, substitutionary forgiveness, intolerance, eternal punishments, and humble worship are all beneath the dignity of intelligent human beings. They are barbaric ideas for primitive cultures cowering in fear and ignorance.

Do you see why I do not respect the biblical message? It is an insulting bag of nonsense. You have every right to torment yourself with such insanity but leave me out of it. I have better things to do with my life.

BIBLE GOSSIP

Form circles with 15 to 30 people in each group. Each person needs paper. The first person, using a Bible, writes one not-so-well-known verse and passes it with the pen to the next person. He reads the verse, destroys the original, rewrites it from memory, passes his copy and the pen to the next person, etc., on down the line. The object is to discover how near the original the last copy will be. This shows in essence, the method of transmitting Scripture through the centuries. This could be an eye opener as to the necessity for memorizing Scriptures. *Roger Copeland*

LOOK AT THE BOOK

The true/false statements on page 46 can be very effective in helping your young people determine their attitudes about the Bible and in helping you discover what your group thinks of the Bible.

Jim Kirkpatrick

AN ORIGINAL DISCOVERY

In order to illustrate how errors were made in the copying of the biblical documents and how textual scholars discover what must have been the original text through study of these copies, give students the following problem to solve during class time. A quotation taken from a text is copied onto a sheet of paper. Five more copies, each with a different copying error, are made on separate sheets. Each sheet is numbered on the back for identification. These six sheets are then distributed to the class members and read aloud, comparisons and contrasts being noted. Then the class works with these documents as follows:

1. Arranges the documents into similar pairs (noting that no two are identical).

2. Determines which one of each pair was a copy of the other.

3. Compares the differences among all six and among the three pairs, noting how these differences might have occurred.

4. Tries to determine which is the original document.

Here are six sample statements with explanatory comments:

1. The story was in German. More than 700 copies of the story, or parts of it, have survived. These copies are also in German.

2. The story was written in German. More than 700 copies of the story, or of parts of the story, or of parts of it, have survived to our time. These copies are also in German.

3. The story was written in German. More than 70 copies of the story, or of parts of it, have survived to our time. These copies are also in German.

4. The story was in German. More than 700 copies of the story, or of parts of it, had survived. These copies are also in German.

5. The story was written in German. More than 700 copies of the story, or of parts of it, have survived to our time. These copies are also in German.

6. The story was written in German. More than 70 copies of it have survived to our time. These copies are also in German.

1. Omits "written" and "to our time." Is paired with #4, which is a copy of it.

2. Repeats third line of the original, "of the story, or of parts" (see #5). This is paired with the original, #5.

3. Omits zero from 700 making it 70. Paired with #6, which is a copy of it.

4. Omits "written" and "to our time." Also changes "have" to "had." Paired with #1. It is a copy of #1 since #1 retains "have" from the original.

5. This is the original. It is paired with #2, although #1 and #3 are also close copies of it.

6. Omits third line of the original, #5, "of the story, or of parts." Also omits zero from 700; thus it is paired with #3. This is a copy of #3 since #3 contains the third line of the original.

To clarify the differences among the documents, have class members diagram the relationships among the documents as follows:
This kind of study will convince them of the exact-

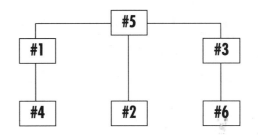

ing work of scholars in this field. It will assure them of the reliability of today's reconstructed Greek and Hebrew texts. And it may even excite students to investigate this subject further on a level usually reserved for seminar work.

For large classes this project can be expanded by developing more copies with different types of errors. Or students might examine the documents in teams. *David Cassel*

LOOK AT THE BOOK

True	False	1.	The Bible is a record of man's search for God.
True	False	2.	The Bible is like a scientific textbook when it describes the origin of the world.
True	False	3.	The Bible is primarily a factual history of the Jewish people.
True	False	4.	The Bible contains detailed answers to all of man's questions.
True	False	5.	The Bible needs to be interpreted literally.
True	False	6.	The main thrust of the biblical witness is the description of ethical norms (what is right and what is wrong).
True	False	7.	Every part of the Bible has the same level of importance as every other part.
True	False	8.	One needs to read the Bible as a spectator rather than as a participant.
True	False	9.	The Bible was written and compiled all at once.
True	False	10.	All the writings in the Bible are a response to God's activity and concern for his people.
True	False	11.	The Bible can prove the existence of God.
True	False	12.	A person's job in studying the Bible is to learn to ask the right questions.
True	False	13.	The Bible is a recital of history without interruption.
True	False	14.	There is no other truth about God than what is disclosed in the Bible.
True	False	15.	The Old Testament has no relevance for today.
True	False	16.	The Bible is basically one story...that of God's search for communion with man.

Group Story

This idea can help kids appreciate the fact that although the Bible took 40 authors and over 1,500 years to write, it has an amazing unity. This in itself is one evidence of God's hand in the work. Prepare some index cards, as many as there are people in the group. Number them consecutively. On

the first card write, "Once upon a time..." On the last card, write, "And then..." at the top, and "The End." at the bottom. On all the other cards, write "And then..." on the top. Distribute the cards randomly making sure that each person has one.

Next tell the kids to write a portion of a story on their card. They should use their imaginations and write anything they want that would make up part of a good story. When they are finished, the cards are collected, put in order, and the story is read. The result will be a very funny but very disjointed story. Talk about how the Bible had many authors, yet it tells a single story of salvation.

David Farnum

Hidden Treasures

Here's a creative way to allow your group to understand the value of God's wisdom. Before they arrive for Bible study, hide money somewhere in the room. Open the Bible study with prayer. Then tell them that money is hidden in the room and whoever finds it can keep it. Of course, the higher the denomination, the harder the teens will look. When the money is found, take your Bibles and turn to Proverbs 2. It will cause you all to think about how diligently we search the Scriptures as compared to how diligently we're willing to look for "hidden treasures." *Dave Stevens*

Life Got You Puzzled?

After your teens work their way through this idea, they'll be better able to grasp why Scripture is so important.

Split them into groups of four or five, and give each group a jigsaw puzzle to assemble—only, unknown to them, throw into each box some extra pieces from an additional yet similar puzzle. Withhold the box tops. Give each group space to work, and then watch the frustration grow until they realize that there are extra, unusable pieces.

Eventually they'll sort out the different pieces and complete the puzzle. Then discuss these questions:

• How did you feel while you tried to place the unusable pieces?
• Did the unusable pieces make the competition extremely difficult or slightly difficult?
• Did you feel pressure to compete with the other groups?
• How do you think this activity relates to the Christian life?

Make sure kids understand the relationship between this activity and the Christian life. Just as the unusable pieces complicated the task and frustrated or angered the participants, obstacles and problems can make the Christian life more difficult and puzzling. Christians must take the time to sort out and deal with these obstacles. The Bible can show us how to deal best with the problems. Christians who don't rely on Scripture for guidance are merely beating their heads against the wall while trying to cram pieces from two different puzzles into a single picture. It just doesn't work.

Verses for further discussion: 2 Timothy 3:16-17; Matthew 4:1-11; John 1:14-18. *Dave Carver*

BODY OF CHRIST

Pentagon

This game is not only fun to play, but is also excellent as a simulation game to teach the interdependence of members of the body of Christ.

Divide into any number of teams, with six

people on each team. Each team will have five players and one runner. The five players are seated in a pentagon-shaped arrangement with approximately 10 feet separating each player. The runner is in the center.

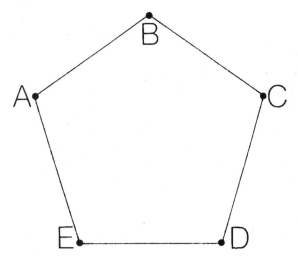

A deck of ordinary playing cards is shuffled and the five players each receive a card. They are to keep the cards concealed and not reveal to anyone which card they have. The object of the game is for each player to learn what cards the other players on his team have, through a process of note-passing. No one may tell another player what card he has. He must write notes. No talking is allowed or the team is disqualified or penalized.

Each player has a scratch pad with plenty of note paper and a pencil. He may only communicate directly with the players to either side of him. For example, A may communicate with B and E, B may communicate with A and C, etc. He must remain seated at all times and give his note to the runner, who delivers everyone's notes back and forth. Each note should state who is sending it and to whom:

To B:
I have the King of Clubs.
From A.

When a player writes a note, he raises his hand until the runner picks the note up and delivers it to whomever it is to. He may only send one note at a time and each note may only give or ask

information concerning one player at a time. In other words, a note cannot say "B has the Jack of Hearts, C has the two of Clubs, and E has the six of Diamonds." That message would require three notes. Once a note has been read and/or answered, it is discarded (wadded up and thrown on the floor).

Each player should be keeping a record of information that he receives. He should have a piece of paper with the following list:

A-
B-
C-
D-
E-

As soon as the list is complete and he knows which cards all of the other four players have, he stands up. While standing, he may still give and receive notes to assist other team members who haven't yet finished. The first team to get all five members standing is the winner, unless someone's information in incorrect. Each person's list must be checked for errors.

This game can be played with more players per team, which will make it longer, or it can be played in different arrangements. One alternative is as follows:

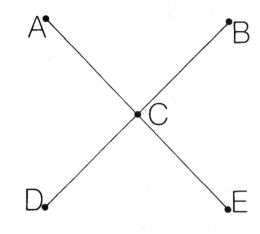

In this variation, the time to complete the game is shorter and the player in the center (C) is very busy, while the other players don't participate as much, since they can only communicate with one person. C can communicate with everybody.

Real names can be used instead of letters of the alphabet. A discussion can follow based on related Scripture, such as 1 Corinthians 12:12-27. In the body of Christ, we all have an equally important part as members of the body. *Jim Olia*

BODY LANGUAGE

Lay a large piece of cardboard cut in the shape of the human body, minus the head, on the floor. Then have the kids, equipped with colored marking pens, choose a part of the body that they feel represents them. They then write on that part of the body their name, or a symbol, or a phrase that relates to their choice. After everyone is finished, each person shares why they chose the part of the body they did and the meaning of the symbol or phrase that related to their choice. At the end of the meeting, you can tape the body to a door and add a cut-out head of Christ. This can be very effective during a discussion of the Church, the body of Christ, and 1 Corinthians 12:12-21. *Richard Young*

POOLING RESOURCES GAME

The following is a simple simulation which teaches the value of working together and pooling resources to accomplish a task. First distribute Tinker Toys to the group, giving each person an equal number of parts—each person should receive only a half dozen or so. Then ask each person to make something. Many will find it difficult due to lack of adequate parts.

Next, get them into groups of from four to 10. Have each group make something with its Tinker Toys. When the groups are finished, allow them to describe their creations with everyone.

Then discuss what happened. Was it easier to make something alone or together with others? Why? What does this tell us about bringing our resources together for a common cause? What happened in the group? What kind of process went on in the decision making? *Charles Stewart*

THE TIE THAT BINDS

Have all the kids stand in a circle. Any group up to 30 will work. Take a long, thick piece of rope or cord and loop it around each kid as in the following illustration. Have them move close together and be sure there is no slack between them. With no explanation of the purpose or point, have each kid take a large step backward one at a time. Go all the way around the circle. (Normally, someone about halfway around will get the bright idea to give a good squeeze to the ones next to him; allow this.) When everyone has stepped back, have the kids drop the rope and sit down.

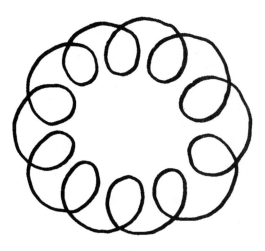

Discuss these questions:

- **When you stepped back, what happened to you and to the ones around you?**
- **What happened when the people next to you stepped back?**
- **What part did the rope play in this experience?**

Now talk about the tie that binds—our love for one another (see John 13:35). One observation that comes across clearly is this: When someone tries to break from fellowship, our love as a group should always hold him in. Close by singing "Blest Be the Tie That Binds." *Steven Robinson*

BODY BALLOON BURST

Here's a fun way to kick off a discussion on the body of Christ, the church, or spiritual gifts.

Randomly assign each person one of the parts of the body listed below. One way to do this

49

with larger groups is to use birthdays (months) or last name initials that correspond to these parts of the body. ("If your last name begins with A through E, then you are a right hand.")

Here are the corresponding motions or gestures for each part of the body:

- Right hands raise and wave their right hands.
- Left hands raise and wave their left hands.
- Right feet hop on their right feet.
- Left feet hop on their left feet.
- Mouths yell.
- Torsos do the twist.

When the signal to go is given, each person performs the motion for his or her part of the body in an attempt to attract other body parts and form a complete, five-person body. No other talking is allowed during this part of the game. Kids must form a group of six—a complete body, including a right and left hand, a right and left foot, a mouth, and a torso.

After the group of six is together, the two feet carry one of the hands to the leader where the hand is given a balloon. The hand—still being carried by the feet—takes the balloon back to the group where the mouth must blow it up. But the mouth cannot touch it; the hands must hold it for the mouth. After the mouth inflates the balloon, the hands tie it off and place it on a chair—at which time the torso sits on it and pops it. The first team to pop its balloon successfully is the winner.

This active and exciting game is a simple yet effective way to show how the various parts of the body must work together in order to accomplish a common goal.

Kool-Aid Koinonia

Here's another idea that can be used to illustrate how each member of the body of Christ is important.

Select three volunteers. Have volunteer 1 wear nose plugs and loosely tie his hands behind his back. Blindfold volunteer 2, place a large thin bandage over her mouth, and loosely tie her hands behind her back. Also blindfold volunteer 3, have him wear nose plugs, and loosely cover his mouth—making sure he can breath comfortably.

Place three drinking glasses on a table. One glass contains Kool-Aid or punch, another contains colored water and looks identical to the Kool-Aid, and the third is empty.

The object is for the three volunteers to work together to accomplish the following:

1. Decide which glass is filled with genuine Kool-Aid.
2. Pour the Kool-Aid into the empty glass.
3. Serve the Kool-Aid to volunteer 1.

Since 1 is the only one who can speak, he calls out instructions to the other two. Volunteer 2 is the only one who can smell, so she sniffs the glasses to determine which glass contains the Kool-Aid. Volunteer 3 is the only one with hands free, so he pours the Kool-Aid and serves it to 1.

One entertaining way to do this is to have three groups of three try it, bringing them in one group at a time before the rest of group. When they come in explain what they have to do and see which group can complete the task in the shortest time. *J. Allen Eubanks*

Making It on Your Own

You can't make it in the Christian life solo—that's the point of this origami activity. Make sure you can make this origami successfully before attempting it with your group.

As kids enter the room, hand them a set of directions (see page 51), a square sheet of paper, and your comment: "Read and follow directions." The first dozen steps are easy. After that, guided practice is required. When your kids near the frustration point, help them understand the directions and how to implement them with their own papers. The result is an origami flapping bird.

So it is with our faith. We find much of it understandable, but it is helpful to interact with other Christians in order to get through tough, confusing times, to understand the more complicated biblical concepts, or to gain a new appreciation for Scripture or a different point of view. *David Washburn*

The Group Is You

To demonstrate to your students that their spiritual-

Making It On Your Own
ORIGAMI FLAPPING BIRD

KEY: FOLD — — — — REVERSE FOLD ▷ DRAWING FOLLOWED BY ↻ MEANS TURN MODEL OVER

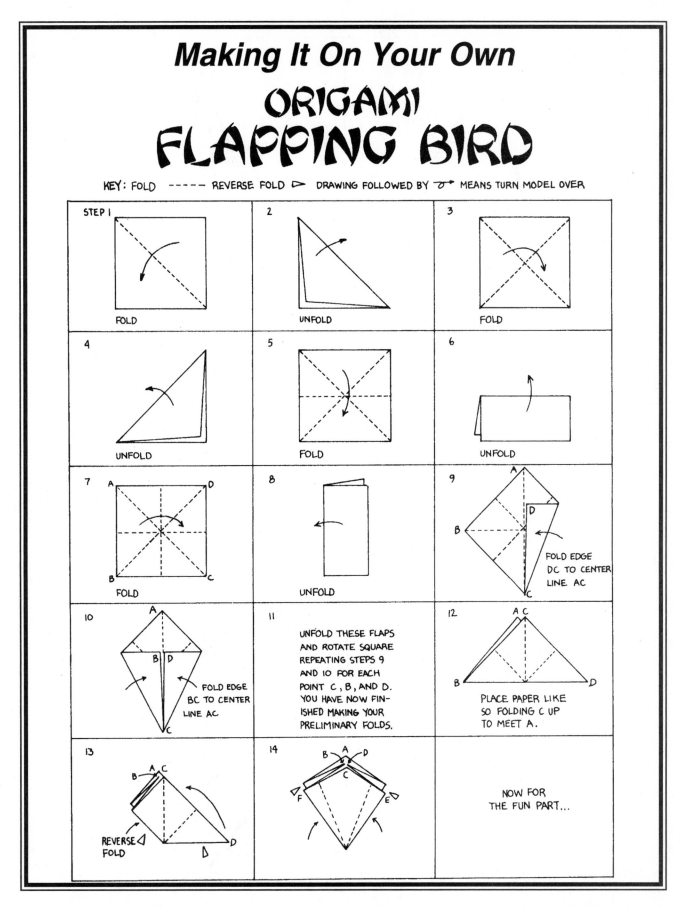

STEP 1 — FOLD

2 — UNFOLD

3 — FOLD

4 — UNFOLD

5 — FOLD

6 — UNFOLD

7 — FOLD

8 — UNFOLD

9 — FOLD EDGE DC TO CENTER LINE AC

10 — FOLD EDGE BC TO CENTER LINE AC

11 — UNFOLD THESE FLAPS AND ROTATE SQUARE REPEATING STEPS 9 AND 10 FOR EACH POINT C, B, AND D. YOU HAVE NOW FINISHED MAKING YOUR PRELIMINARY FOLDS.

12 — PLACE PAPER LIKE SO FOLDING C UP TO MEET A.

13 — REVERSE FOLD

14 — NOW FOR THE FUN PART...

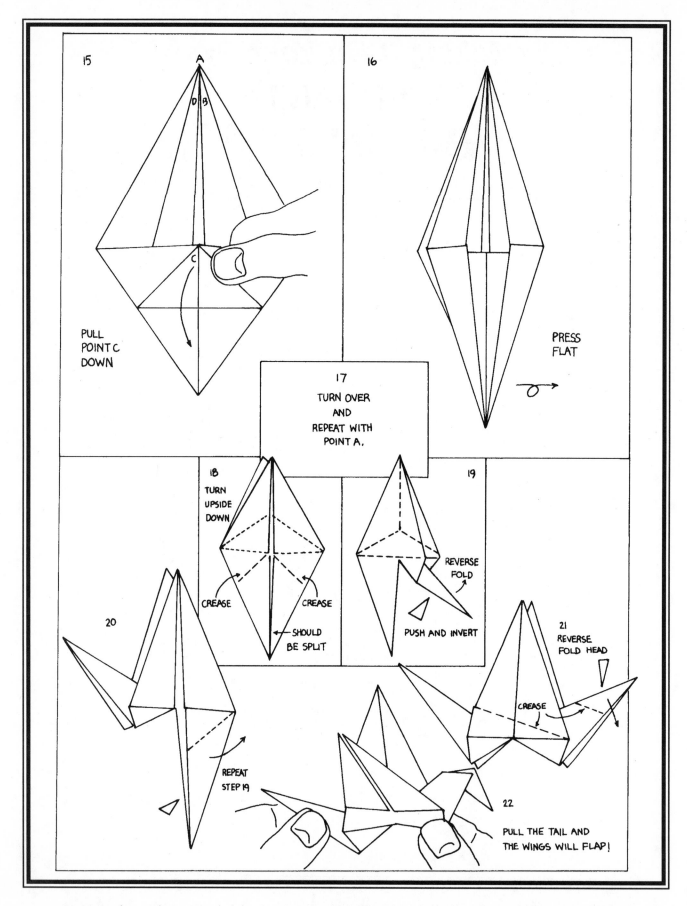

15

A
D B

C

PULL
POINT C
DOWN

16

PRESS
FLAT

17

TURN OVER
AND
REPEAT WITH
POINT A.

18
TURN
UPSIDE
DOWN

CREASE   CREASE

←SHOULD
BE SPLIT

19

REVERSE
FOLD

PUSH AND INVERT

20

REPEAT
STEP 19

21
REVERSE
FOLD HEAD

CREASE

22

PULL THE TAIL AND
THE WINGS WILL FLAP!

ity as a group only reflects their individual spirituality, pass out pencils and note cards for them to rate their group spiritually. They should rank their group from 1 to 10 on several questions, such as:

- Is there a Christlike love and concern within our group?
- Do visitors and new members feel welcome?
- Are Bible study and prayer high priorities for our group?
- If you were a visitor, would you want to be a part of this group?

Collect the cards when they're finished rating the group. Then pass out another card to each student and ask the same or similar questions again, this time adapting them to individuals; for example, "Do you personally have a Christlike love for others?"

When finished gather this set of cards. Calculate the averages of both sets of questions, then compare the two averages. The two figures are often fairly close to each other—a mere five percent difference is not unusual. Pursue the idea in a discussion that their unity with each other depends on their personal walks with Christ. *Tom Daniel*

Jigsaw Puzzle

Take a picture of the youth group. Cut it up into as many pieces as there are people. Send each youth a piece of the puzzle with instructions to bring it to the next meeting. The number of pieces missing dramatizes the completeness or incompleteness of the body of Christ.
• **A Puzzling Church.** If you liked Jigsaw Puzzle, you'll love this elaboration of the idea.

Set up tables around the room. Divide your group into teams of three to six people, and provide each team with a 250 to 300 piece jigsaw puzzle. All of the puzzles should have the same number of pieces but should be of different scenes. Announce that the first team to complete its puzzle will win a prize.

After 10 minutes or so, announce a team shift (actually, the first of three—but don't let on that there will be any more). Gauge the timing of the subsequent shifts on the speed at which the puzzles are being completed.

—**Shift 1.** Each team moves to another puzzle, but everyone must work without talking among themselves.

—**Shift 2.** The teams move to yet a different puzzle—but just before they rotate, you remove the puzzle box with the picture on it. They may resume talking to one another, however.

—**Shift 3.** This time everyone scrambles themselves into new teams as they each move to a puzzle they haven't worked on yet. Return the puzzle boxes to each table as they're settling in.

As soon as the first puzzle is completed, stop the activity and award the prize. Conclude with a discussion of the following:

- Reaping what you have not sown
- The importance of the Bible and the life of Jesus as a model for Christian living
- Division of duties in the body of Christ
- Unfinished business at the second coming of Christ
- Commitment to ministry and the church in a transient culture
- Competition/cooperation
- Leadership in the body of Christ
- Unity and diversity
- The task of the church
- Denominations

Jim Hudson and David Shaw

Puzzling a Youth Group

Here's a group-building exercise. Purchase at an art store a large piece of bristle board that is mounted on ¼-inch-thick Styrofoam. Before the session cut the Styrofoam with a sharp blade into enough puzzle pieces for the number of kids expected to attend. Make it as difficult as you wish.

When the kids arrive ask them to each decorate with marking pens one piece of the puzzle. (Use fruit-scented markers for more sensory appeal!) Decorations should include the artist's name, age, grade, school, and a drawing of a favorite activity (or any other aspect of identity you may choose).

When all have completed their pieces, put the puzzle together. Add in any blank pieces to represent the potential for new members. Take a picture of the finished puzzle with the contributors lying around it. *Susan and David Johnson*

TARGET TOGETHERNESS

To show that the church needs the talents of all of its members to succeed in completing God's mission for it, let the kids experience depending upon each other. They'll learn it's not always easy to work together, but when everyone persists in contributing to the effort, their goal can be achieved.

For each group you'll need three Ping-Pong balls, three wide rubber bands, and two blindfolds. You'll also need masking tape, Dixie cups, and one table for every three groups. Set up pyramids of stacked Dixie cups on tables as targets for the teams.

To start, divide the group into threesomes. Ask each trio to construct a slingshot by tying the rubber bands together and taping a pocket on the center rubber band. Assign body parts to the three teammates—one is the eyes, one is the right arm, and one is the left arm. Blindfold the right arm and left arm, and give the right arm the slingshot.

Play begins with all the right arms sitting on the floor facing the table and holding the slingshot with both hands over their heads. All the left arms kneel behind the right arms, loading the slingshots with Ping-Pong balls, and firing at the targets. All eyes stand behind the left arms and verbally direct them in aiming for the targets. The first group to hit a stack of cups wins that round.

After three shots, allow the group members to switch roles within their own group. Go several rounds and keep a running total of hits. *Doug Partin*

COOKIE BAKE

Illustrate how believers need each other while creating the evening's snack—make chocolate chip cookies.

Write on poster board a recipe for mouth-watering chocolate chip cookies, and hang it out-side the church kitchen door. Gather all the ingredients needed to make the cookies, as well as the utensils you need—bowl, mixing spoon, cookie sheets, pot holders, metal spatulas. Divide participants into groups of four, and assign one person in each group one of the following roles.

• **Messenger** is the only one who can look at the recipe. Messenger can neither speak nor walk, however. Messenger writes out each step at the proper time, and Guide carries Messenger to deliver the writing to Encourager.

• **Arms** is the blindfolded player who mixes ingredients together.

• **Guide** carries Messenger to deliver the recipe, but Guide's mouth is taped shut.

• **Encourager**, seated in a chair through the whole process, receives written recipe steps from Messenger and tells Arms what to do to make the cookies. Encourager inspires all the team's participants to work fast and efficiently.

After each team mixes up a batch of dough, everyone forms and bakes the cookies. While the cookies are baking, read and discuss 1 Corinthians 12:12-31 (spiritual gifts given for the common good). Conclude by eating the cookies fresh from the oven. *Glenn Balzer*

CHRISTIAN LIFE AND CHRISTIANITY

BOWLING TOURNEY DEVOTIONAL

Use the handout on page 55 after your next bowling event. *Mark Adams*

RACE OF LIFE

This game doubles as a parable. It speaks to the common response of teens to the demands of discipleship: "If all I need to gain eternal life is to claim Jesus as my Savior before I die, then why shouldn't I just have the best time I can and save religion for the deathbed?"

Explain to the group that they're going to race to a determined finish line. They all must start

STRIKES, SPARES, SPLITS, AND GUTTER BALLS

Ever notice how bowling is a lot like the Christian life?

❖ ❖ ❖

• **STRIKES** occur in a Christian's life during times of great spiritual highs (like retreats and youth rallies). Because of those times, we follow through in our determination to put God first in our lives. Life actually becomes abundant! (Read Matthew 6:33 for more about this.)

❖ ❖ ❖

• **SPARES** usually follow shortly after the strikes. You leave a mountain-top experience committed to daily Bible study and prayer, and you keep rolling those strikes—at least for a week or so. Then you let yourself slip into old habits, and pretty soon your abundant life starts becoming meager again. If you realize your mistake and put God first again—start spending time with him again—abundant life can resume, kind of like picking up a spare. (Read John 10:10 to see the kind of life God wants us to have.)

• **SPLITS** occur when a seemingly impossible task confronts you. You're going along the best you can, but then you think, "I can't do this." Then you realize that on your own you can't, but with God you can. When we wise up and rely on his strength instead of our own, we find we can complete the task. (See Luke 1:37.)

❖ ❖ ❖

• **GUTTER BALLS** are what you get when you're too close to the edge and your momentum carries you into the gutter. Sometimes we Christians push God farther and farther from the center of our lives. We reserve him for Sundays alone. We wander from his will during the week, and sooner or later the inevitable happens—we tumble over the edge of association with the wrong crowd into participation with what they do. We've conformed to the standards of the world. (Paul warns about this in Romans 12:1-2.)

Well, fellow holy roller, it's my prayer that your Christian life will be full of strikes and spares—but mostly strikes!

when the whistle blows, must walk (not run), and must freeze when the whistle blows a second time.

Make it equally clear, too, that they *may* cheat.

- **First Round.** Blow the whistle to start the race. When a few reach the finish line, blow the whistle a second time. Now announce that those who cheated (either by running or by not freezing in time) are hunchbacked. For the remaining rounds they must walk with their hands on their knees. Announce to the kids who made it to the finish line fairly that, because they seem to have a natural advantage, they must be handicapped—so they also will have to walk hunchbacked (one hand on a knee) for the remaining rounds.

- **Second Round.** Repeat the race and follow the same procedure. Only this time, however, the cheaters and the winners become crippled—that is, they have to hold onto one foot and hop on the other for the remaining rounds. Those who are already hunchbacked must keep one hand on a knee as well as hold one foot with the other hand.

- **Third Round.** Repeat the race. This time the cheaters and winners become blind and have to close their eyes for the fourth and final round.

- **Fourth Round.** After this round ask everyone who is not hunchbacked, crippled, or blind to come forward. These are the actual winners. Explain that the objective was never to be first to the finish line; the objective was to finish the race as a whole person.

Explain to the kids the save-it-for-the-deathbed approach to Christianity. Read them the quotation from the first paragraph of this idea, then ask them, "How does this game answer this question?" First of all, what may appear to be the obvious objective in life is not the real objective. The real objective in life is not to satisfy our appetites for sex, money, or power, but to be a whole person. Second, sin cripples us. We suffer from the guilt, shame, and consequences of our sins in this life regardless of the life to come. Sin keeps us from reaching the real goal in life.

When the kids respond, "But you said we could cheat," explain that the game also illustrates free will—we are free to live in the manner we choose. Finally, you may want to add that sin inhibits us from reaching even the illusory goals—overindulging our appetites brings us to a point of diminishing returns. *Andrew Parker*

DRIVING LESSON

Communicating the lordship of Christ to high school freshmen and sophomores by giving them a chance behind your car's wheel really gets the point across. You will, of course, need to get parents' permission before this event.

While the youths are participating in some social activity inside the church, one by one take the freshmen and sophomores outside. Give each student the keys to your car, which is parked just outside the door.

Explain the activity to each student:

I want you to drive my car around the parking lot for a few minutes, going no faster than 25 mph. Once you and I are inside the car, however, I am officially ignorant of how to operate and drive it, so asking for my advice won't help. The only time I will interfere is if you are about to hit something or you lose control.

(It's a riot watching these younger high schoolers—most of whom have never driven before—try to find the ignition, the lights, figure out how to engage the transmission, etc.)

Halfway around the parking lot, explain that you aren't doing this because you want to be the coolest youth pastor of all time (though, of course, you are). Tell them something like this:

I'm a better driver than you are, and I like being in control. It's difficult for me to let an inexperienced and nervous person like you drive. Likewise, God is better at directing your life than you are, and he would rather you gave him control since you are inexperienced and unsure of life's road. That's the real sign of letting Christ be Lord of your life—when you let him be in control.

After each student parks as close as possible to the original parking spot (a laugh in itself), pray together and hand the student a 3x5 note card with a key glued to it. The card lists verses about the importance of giving God control each day. Ask each student to keep secret from the rest of the group what happened outside.

This activity can be a success (but not a smashing one, we hope) and can stimulate great group discussions after you've done this with several students. *Kevin Conklin*

HELP WANTED

This idea will get your group thinking about the kind of people God is looking for. Read a sampling from your newspaper's help-wanted section to your group. Then have kids write out their own help-wanted ads as if they were written by God and run in the local newspaper. The ads could be titled "Help Wanted" or "Position Available" and contain a description of the kind of person God wants. Here's a sample ad:

HELP WANTED

Need believers who are responsible, loving, understanding, willing to sacrifice themselves for others. False pretenses are not welcome. Applicant must be loyal, faithful. Great benefits. Life insurance paid in full. Please call me at B-I-B-L-E anytime; I'm always there. An equal opportunity employer.

When ads are completed, have kids turn over their papers and write their resumes to qualify for the job. Or post all the ads on a bulletin board and have kids write a reply to the one that most appeals to them. Make sure they include a note to God explaining why they are qualified for the job. Invite volunteers to read their ads and replies to the group or collect the ads and replies and read them aloud to the group.

You could follow this with a study on God's grace and how he accepts us as his children unconditionally (Ephesians 2:8-9). Or, follow with a lesson on being available to God, explaining how God can use all of us regardless of our backgrounds or past failures. *Phil Print*

PARABLES FOR TODAY

Here is a study on the parables of Christ that allows kids to create a parable of their own. To begin have the kids read a parable from Scripture, like the parable of the sower in Mark 4:3-9. Then discuss the following questions. They can be presented and discussed orally with the entire group, or you might want to print the questions up and have the kids write out their answers and discuss in small groups.

• What is a parable?
• What does the parable of the sower try to teach?
• Why do you think Jesus chose to teach in parables instead of some other way?
• What advantage does a parable have over other ways of teaching?
• What other parables do you know from the Bible? From elsewhere?

The next step is to challenge the kids to come up with a parable of their own—now that they understand something about the nature of parables. Give them the following six steps (put them up on a blackboard or have them printed up so that they can be passed out) and let them work on their parable for 10 minutes or so. Let kids know that their parables don't have to be very long or complicated or heavy. In fact, the simpler, the better.

1. Pick an object or idea for your parable (Hint: a seed).
2. Think how this object relates to some truth God gives us. Use as many ways of showing that truth with your object as possible.
3. Now write out your parable and title it.
4. Have your object with you (if possible) when it is your turn to read your parable, to use as a visual aid to your listeners.
5. Think of some questions you can ask the listeners to see if they understood your parable.
6. Gather back with the group, and wait for your turn to read. Listen to the others.

After the parables have been written, allow the kids to share them with each other and to discuss each one briefly. You'll find this to be a great way to encourage creativity and to provide some excellent learning, too. *Jeff Pool*

SYMBOL WALK

The New Testament Gospels use various symbols and metaphors to explain spiritual realities. The following activity is designed to help your kids understand these different symbols.

You will need seven rooms (Sunday school rooms are ideal) and the following items: a lighted candle, a few ounces of salt, a bowl filled with water, mustard seeds or other small seeds, a sewing needle, a loaf of bread, and a couple of apples sliced into sections. Put one item in each of the rooms.

Provide paper cups in the room with the water.

Divide the kids into smaller groups of four to six people. Make sure each group has an adult sponsor. Each group must visit each room, study the specified object in it, and exhaustively describe the object. The sponsor should make sure that kids describe only the objects, not their uses or any meaning they might hold. Students can use all of their senses (taste, smell, etc.) in describing the object. "The pile of particles is white; each particle is very small; all of the particles appear to be the same size; the individual particles are not pure white but are almost transparent; there is a shiny quality to the particles; the particles feel hard; the shape of the particles is square; their taste is not sweet; the pile does not have an odor."

After the description is complete, the sponsor should read the verse that uses the object as a metaphor. The small group can then spend a few minutes reflecting on why that particular object was used in the verse. When finished groups can then move on to the next room and begin the description-reflection process again. Here are some of the symbols you might wish to use:

Symbol	Verse
Light (candle)	John 1:1-9
Salt	Matthew 5:13
Water	Matthew 3:13-17
Mustard seeds	Matthew 17:20
Needle	Matthew 19:23-24
Bread	John 6:50-51
Apple	Matthew 7:16-17

To close the session bring the groups together to reread the verses and to discuss the meaning of the objects used in the verses. Here are some possible questions you might want to use, along with your own:

• Which object made the biggest impression to you?
• What new things did you learn about the objects as you described them?
• Why do you think symbols are used in the Bible?
• What are some of the other symbols and metaphors that could be used in place of the ones in the verses.

Vicky Roark and Sam Deputy

THE SERMON OF THE MOUSE

The article on page 59 can be read aloud to the group or it can be printed and passed out to each person. It raises some important issues concerning the church and should be discussed using the questions that follow or others that you may want to add.

Questions for discussion:

• What parallels, if any, do you see between amusements like Disneyland and the organized church?
• Analyze the statement, "Give the illusion of great risk, but make everything safe."
  – Are there any risks involved in being a Christian today?
  – Does modern Christianity really cost the Christian anything?
  – Can you think of any examples of the church creating an illusion of risk?
  – How, if at all, does a church make people safe?
• Analyze the statement, "Entertain the people."
  – How do churches entertain their people?
  – Should Christianity and the Church be entertaining?
  – React to this statement: "People today must be entertained. After all, they have become sophisticated by watching the professional entertainment on television and at the movies. The church is competing for a person's time and attention and must give them something to make them want to come. After they get there, then they can be given spiritual content.
• Analyze the statement, "Make everything look religious."
  – Define religious.
  – What do you think Mickey Mouse meant by religious?
• Analyze the statement, "Pretend there are no problems."
  – Do you think the church should admit to having problems? Should the pastor? Should the people?
  – How can a church pretend it doesn't have any problems?
  – If Christianity is true, then don't problems raise doubts in the minds of searching unbelievers?

Dave Phillips

BETHANY CHURCH

This simulation deals with church structure, the mission of the church, unity in the church, and a host of other issues as well. Be sure plenty of time is avail-

The Sermon of the Mouse

The day had finally arrived. Everyone in the congregation was waiting expectantly. The negotiations had taken months, but finally everything had been worked out. It wasn't every congregation in the country that could have an opportunity like this. It was a rare visit from a very well-known celebrity.

The pastor and his guest mounted the platform. The first hymn was sung. Then the pastor rose. "I'm sure everyone is aware who our guest speaker is this morning," he said.

Aware? How could anyone help being aware? There were posters all over town. There was a big yellow and black banner stretched across the entry to the parking lot. Seating in the sanctuary had been on a reservation basis with preferential treatment given to members in good standing of the congregation. An overflow crowd was watching the service on closed circuit television. Everybody knew about it.

"It isn't often," said the pastor, "that we have an opportunity to meet someone who has become a legend in his own time. Starting back in the bleak years of the depression with a shoestring budget and a very simple plan, our guest, with hard work and contagious enthusiasm, built an empire for himself that rivals that of Howard Hughes. His name is a household word, he is admired by young and old alike, and he has even survived his mentor. He reigns over a multi-million dollar business venture that was so successful in Southern California that he established an even more spectacular venture in Florida. By now, I'm sure you know who I am talking about. We are so honored to have Mickey Mouse with us today to share with us the secrets of Disneyland's success with the hope that our church will be stimulated and helped by his story."

A hush came over the congregation as this famous mouse rose to his feet, cleared his throat, and began his sermon.

"Thank you for inviting me to come to your church. I must admit at first I was surprised that a church would ask me to give a sermon. Oh, I have been invited to Sunday school contests where they give each new person a Mickey Mouse hat and expect me to shake hands with everyone and act funny, but a sermon is something new.

"But after I thought about it, I realized that maybe Disneyland and the church do have a lot in common and as I began to organize my thoughts, I saw how ingenious it was to invite me to share. I really believe that if your church were to apply our principles you could become as successful as Disneyland.

"First, make sure your enterprise seems exciting, even dangerous, but be quick to let your people know that there really is no danger involved. Give the illusion of great risk, but make sure everything is perfectly safe.

"Second, admit that you are in the entertainment business. People won't care what you say as long as they're entertained. Keep your people happy. Don't tell them anything negative. And don't make demands on them. Just keep them diverted from the ugly reality of today's world and they will keep coming back for more.

"Third, make everything look religious. Make the religious experience so elaborate, so intricate, so complex that only the professionals can pull it off and all the laymen can do is stand around with their mouths open and watch. People would rather watch an imitation mechanical bird sing than they would a real bird anyway. They would rather watch worship than do it.

"Finally, pretend that there are no problems. At Disneyland we dress our security guards up as smiling rabbits or friendly bears because we don't want anyone's experience at Disneyland to be ruined by the sight of law enforcement personnel. Disguise your problems and failures behind a warm smile and a firm handshake. Leave them at home and let the church be a happy place where there aren't any ugly problems. Just friendly pastors and smiling deacons.

"People today want good, clean entertainment. They want an environment that is safe for children and they want a place that is safe for their family and friends. I am so glad to see that the church is moving in this direction. Thank you and God bless you."

able. It works well with junior highers to adults.

Tell students that they are all members of a fictional church called Bethany Church, which is located in the city of Gitchigumi, in the heart of the downtown area. Gitchigumi has a population of 72,000. The church has a membership of 580 adult members. Although membership has recently been declining, the church is not in serious trouble. It is served by a senior minister, an assistant minister, and a full-time secretary. The church budget is $150,000 per year and was raised last year with some difficulty. Of this total, about $9,000 annually has been allocated to the mission of the church.

(Feel free to use the name and description of your own church here to add realism to this simulation. Adapt the entire simulation, including the proposals and the interest groups, to fit your church.)

Recently a wealthy resident of the community passed away and left $250,000 in cash to the church. The church is now faced with a decision on how to use that money, since the person who left it did not specify how it was to be used. That person did, however, insist that majority vote among church members determine how the money would be used (within a certain time limit)—otherwise the money would be turned over to another charitable organization: the Society for the Preservation of Begonias.

With that in mind, divide the group into a number of interest groups (see page 61). Each interest group is provided with a role identity, an assigned number of votes, and a set of goals for itself. The effectiveness of each group will depend, to a large degree, on the ability of its members to role-play the assigned viewpoints and identity of the group.

After the groups have been assigned, several proposals are presented (see page 62). Each group must decide which one (only one!) of these proposals, if adopted, would provide the kind of addition to the life of Bethany Church that would be desirable by its own standards. Then, participants may devise a strategy for using their group's power or influence to secure the assistance of the other groups in getting their favorite proposal adopted. Participants may also try to block, by any means in line with the identity of their group, the adoption

of proposals that they feel would adversely affect Bethany Church. If none of the proposals are acceptable to the group, group members may suggest alternatives.

Following the simulation, discuss the experience with the entire group. Get students to talk about their feelings about what happened. Tie in this experience with other learning strategies, Bible study, or opportunities for personal growth and commitment. *Malcolm McQueen*

WHO'S WHO—THEN AND NOW

This activity can spark discussion and break the ice. Create two quizzes—place one on each side of the same sheet of paper. The "Who's Who—Now?" quiz consists of 20 or so questions concerning people in your church. Here are some sample questions:

- Who works at Dunkin' Donuts?
- Who is the chairman of our church board?
- Who teaches our sixth grade class?
- Who puts the sermon titles up on the church sign each week?
- Who is in charge of getting the church bus ready for Sunday?

On the other side of the sheet is a second quiz: "Who's Who—Then?" Make sure it has the same number of questions as the first quiz. This quiz is about people in the Bible. Here are some sample questions:

- Who built the first temple in Jerusalem?
- Who led the exodus out of Egypt?
- Who did Jesus raise from the dead in the Gospel of John?
- Who was the first murderer?
- Who took a ride inside a fish?

Have each kid take both quizzes and tally two scores—one point per correct answer. Kids should create a fraction from their scores by placing the score for the first quiz above the score for the second quiz (draw a line between the scores to make it look like a fraction). For instance, a score of 16/19 means 16 correct answers to the quiz about people in the church, and 19 correct answers to the Bible quiz. You will probably notice a variety of scores. Compare and contrast the relative importance of how much we know about people in the

Bethany Church's Interest Groups

Instructions:

1. Divide into assigned groups. You are in _____.
2. Read the description of the group you are representing.
3. Decide how you will role-play that group.
4. Decide which proposals you are in favor of and which you object to.
5. Talk with members of other groups at the designated time to convince them of your argument.
6. Hand in a written ballot as to how you are voting. You may vote either for a proposal or against a proposal. For example, if you have 15 votes, you can cast three votes for the evangelistic crusade, six votes against the day care, and six votes for the building addition.
7. The votes will be tabulated and if a certain proposal has a majority of the votes it will win. If not, another round will be played, following steps 4 through 6.
8. If, at the end of four rounds, no one proposal can be agreed upon, Bethany Church will lose the $250,000 gift, and it will be given to the Society for the Preservation of Begonias.

The Choir. The choir is not the most accessible group in the church, since it is dominated by the members of four or five of the oldest families in the church. To them the worship life of the church is central, and at times, music is the center of that worship. Most of the people are over 45, and most of them are very pious. They are the active core of the pastor's adult Bible study group that meets during the Sunday school hour. *(10 votes)*

Executive Board of Church Women. These officers speak for the concerns of the women's ministries. They are perhaps better educated than the congregation as a whole. All of them are married, most of them are homemakers, and they are quite concerned about the church's ministry to young people and children. *(20 votes)*

The Board. This is a group of men between the ages of 35 and 70. They are entrusted with the responsibility of raising money and supervising the activities of the church. The majority of them are businessmen. A group of professionals is also on the board—a doctor, a lawyer, an engineer, and a college teacher. The group is rather conservative and traditional. *(30 votes)*

Young Adult Discussion Group. This group of post-college married couples and singles is the most lively and most progressive group within the church. This group meets every Sunday night and studies such things as it wishes, emphasizing fellowship, study, and social concern in equal measure. The pastor speaks of this group as the conscience of Bethany, because of its willingness to raise unpopular issues and its general contribution to the liveliness of the church. *(15 votes)*

The Church Staff. Three people make up this group: the senior pastor (age 55), the assistant pastor (29), and the church secretary (who has worked here 15 years—more than either minister). These three people have particular interests and loyalties, but also feel to some extent a responsibility to look out for the general welfare of the church. *(20 votes)*

The Youth Fellowship. This group, made up largely of sons and daughters of church members plus a few of their nonmember friends, meets weekly for fun and discussion. It has recently been developing interest in how the church can be more responsive to community needs, though a few members are pressing for a more personally oriented, evangelical emphasis. *(10 votes)*

Neighborhood and Street People. Though they are not actually members of Bethany Church, these people are interested in the use and purpose of the church. Some of them resent the church's tax exempt status and feel that it owes the community more specific community services. *(5 votes)*

The Proposals of Bethany Church

Proposal 1: **Crusade.** In light of 1) the large number of people who don't attend church in Gitchigumi, and 2) the constant tendency of others in the church to fall away, it is proposed that the whole gift be invested so that it yields $15,000 annually in interest to fund a weeklong evangelistic crusade. This fund would allow the church to obtain a first-rate evangelist, ample radio and TV advertising, and part-time summer help to follow up on new conversions. Special music would also be included.

Proposal 2: **Community service.** In light of the severe economic and social distress of many aged members of the congregation, it is proposed that the $250,000 be the first money to fund construction of low-cost housing and other facilities for those elderly in need.

Proposal 3: **CE building addition.** The $250,000 should be used to finance a modest addition to the current Christian education building that would be helpful to the church in these ways: 1) to relieve overcrowding of current Sunday school classes by constructing six new classrooms; 2) to provide adequate office facilities for the assistant minister; 3) to provide a combination gymnasium/activity room that would be used to build a more active youth program; 4) to provide a prayer chapel for small groups within the church and for individual meditation. Since the property is already owned, it is possible to do this for $250,000.

Proposal 4: **Day-care facility.** Gitchigumi desperately needs more day care for children of working mothers. The Sunday school rooms sit unused throughout the week. For $100,000 these rooms could be equipped to provide a day-care facility for 15 to 30 children. The other $150,000 could be used over several years to finance one full-time professional staff person who, with the help of church volunteers, could staff the program. After a few years fees would help pay for additional staff, thus making it a self-supporting facility. Although this plan would fulfill fewer needs in our own church—although it would certainly bring some families into the church—it would benefit the community, thereby broadening our church's outreach in the community.

Proposal 5: **More staff.** Given the current budget, it would not be possible to hire another minister in the near future. Yet we need a full-time professional to visit the sick and shut-ins and to provide personal and family counseling. This would free our other ministers to do their jobs more vigorously and would lead to the eventual building up of the congregation. With the $250,000 in a savings account drawing interest of $15,000 a year, another minister could be hired.

Proposal 6: **New organ.** The organ in the sanctuary desperately needs to be replaced. The pipes are cracking and there are notes that do not even play. Since the worship service depends on the organ for music, it is imperative that the organ be replaced. This can be done for only $230,000.

Bible and how much we know about people in the church. Is it good to learn all about people in the Bible and not know each other very well? Or vice versa? Is one more important than the other or are they equally important? These questions are both thought-provoking and significant. *Wilber Griffith*

MISSION POSSIBLE

Introduce a Bible study on Christian fellowship and outreach by challenging your group to rediscover and recommit itself to a biblical purpose for its existence. Present the scenario on page 64 in which small groups of students must defend the youth group's existence before the governing body of the church. Emphasize that students must use Scripture to make their points. *Jim Bell*

WORKERS IN THE CHURCH

This is a good small group activity that helps people build positive relationships with each other. It also helps people to see how different they all are, yet how important they are to the whole body of Christ. Give each person a copy of the handout on page 65, and have him write in the names of the people in their group beside each job. After doing so, discussion may follow with each person telling why they made their choices. *Bill O'Connor*

YOUTH GROUP CREEDS

Most church bodies have definite stands on social and moral issues such as marriage, sex, pollution, war, homosexuality, divorce, alcohol, tobacco, euthanasia, abortion, other religions, materialism, and so forth. Have your group write up its own creed or statement of belief on one or more of these topics without knowing the official position of the church. Compare this stance with the church's. This can lead into a discussion of the difference or similarity of the creeds, and also about how such creeds are arrived at. Chances are there will be some arguments over the youth group creed. The students will begin to understand how much harder it is for a whole church to agree on something. *Derek McAleer*

GROUP REVELATION

The Bible study on page 66 will stimulate good discussion. Use it at the end of the year or at a time when you suspect people in your group might be privately dealing with some personal problems. This study provides a good look at Scripture and can be a sound basis for evaluation of your group as well.
Randy Comer

COMMUNICATION

HEARING-AND-SEEING GAME

This is a good exercise that deals with communication. To begin, the instructions on page 67 should be given to each player.

After all have finished, ask for the recorders to report on what they heard. List major ideas. Reread the Scripture passage. To follow up, you may want to assign group projects based on the ideas and probes presented. *John Washburn*

PEOPLE PUZZLE GROUPS

The following is an experiment in communications. First divide your large group up into smaller groups of five. (Pick helpers if people are left over—the ones you think would get the least out of the experiment.) Each group of five gets an envelope with different shapes of the same color in it for each member. Use construction paper to make shapes out of these colors: red, blue, black, yellow, green. Follow the sample on page 68. Each person's envelope contains shapes in one of these colors. The object is to form five rectangles, all of equal length and width. However, you cannot speak. You will need pieces in the other envelopes and others will need your pieces. Follow these steps in putting together the puzzles:
1. No speaking. The only thing you can do is offer one of your pieces of the puzzle to another member. You cannot indicate your need for a particular piece. You may only take a piece if it is offered to you (five to 10 minutes).

Mission Possible

At last week's church board meeting, several members raised some serious questions about First Church's youth ministry:

- Isn't this youth group costing us more than it's really worth?
- Aren't today's kids already so busy with school that they don't need activities piled on at church?
- What is this group accomplishing, anyway?
- Why should there even be a youth group—shouldn't the teenagers be involved in the regular church programs?

No one representing the youth ministry was there to answer these questions, and after 45 minutes of discussion, the board voted that unless someone could present at next month's board meeting a good case for continuing the youth group, the youth ministry will be ended.

The church board is willing to hear from someone who thinks the church's youth ministry is important and worthwhile. Your mission is to prepare a statement to present to the church board, answering their questions and telling why you believe First Church should continue its youth ministry.

_____

_____

_____

_____

_____

_____

_____

_____

_____

_____

_____

WORKERS IN THE CHURCH

The Church Carpenter: A person who knows how to build relationships with others that are solid, secure, and long lasting. _____
_____

The Church Electrician: Someone who adds that extra spark to the life of the church. _____
_____
_____

The Church Engineer: Someone with the ability to plan things and to make sure that it is done right. _____
_____

The Church Baker: The person who adds just the right amount of yeast to every occasion so that it rises successfully. _____
_____

The Church Security Guard: Someone who watches out for the welfare of the church and those in it. A person concerned about the well-being of others. _____
_____
_____

The Church Seamstress: Someone who has the ability to sew the little tears back together. Someone who is always able to patch things up._____
_____

The Church Custodian: A person who always seems willing to do the dirty jobs that no one else wants to do. Someone who always makes things look a little better than they were. _____
_____
_____

The Church Tour Guide: Someone who seems to have the ability to show others the right way to go._____
_____

The Church Attorney: A person who stands up on behalf of others and pleads their cause. One who is concerned with justice and equity. _____
_____

The Church Publicity Agent: Someone so excited about the Christian life that he can't keep quiet about it. _____
_____

Others (write your own) _____
_____

Group Revelation

1. In Revelation 2:1-3:19, we find seven letters to seven churches. Each church has its own merits and problems. If John (in the power of the Holy Spirit) were writing to our group, what would he commend us for?

2. Look over this review of the seven churches that the letters were addressed to (Rev. 2:1-3:19).

   A. Ephesus (2:1-7). A church that was orthodox and doctrinally faithful; yet, it had forgotten its first love for the Savior. Faithful to doctrine, but cold in its practice.

   B. Smyrna (2:8-11). Apparently a small, struggling church. Even though it was pure, it was a suffering assembly.

   C. Pergamum (2:12-17). A church of doctrinal compromise. It had begun to drift from the moorings of biblical truth.

   D. Thyatira (2:18-29). An assembly that tolerated a Jezebel in its midst—a person who was leading people astray and winning a hearing, even though she was a false teacher.

   E. Sardis (3:1-6). A church that was big, impressive, and well-known—but dead.

   F. Philadelphia (3:7-13). The most encouraging of all the churches. She had an open door for opportunity and ministry that God wanted her to use. The church was vital, very alive, and full of potential.

   G. Laodicea (3:14-19). A church that received no commendation, one of lukewarm indifference. It was neither hot nor cold, neither dead nor zealous, just bland and tasteless.

3. Which church is most like our group, and why?

4. Pray with a partner now for areas in which we are weak. Jot some of these down.

5. Write a sentence or two of appreciation for your youth leaders and share it with them today.

HEARING AND SEEING GAME

Get into groups of three. Listen to a song that deals with communication. "Sounds of Silence," by Simon and Garfunkel (Columbia Records No. CL2469), is an old-but-still-applicable example. Read the lyrics to the song. Then read to yourself Matthew 13:10-16.

Your group is composed of three people. Each of you will eventually assume the following roles.

- **The Communicator.** Your job will be to tell the other two members of your group your responses about the questions below. Be honest. If you don't like the questions, form new ones that you can respond to. Here are the questions:

  1. What are your immediate feelings about the song?

  2. What is its central point?

  3. What is it saying about communication?

  4. Do you see any relationship between the song and the Scripture verses?

  5. How can we really understand each other?

  6. In what ways can you improve communication in class? At home? At school? In town?

- **The Interviewer.** You should try to help the "Communicator" in what he or she is trying to say. Ask questions related to the questions above. If you see something in the background to what they are saying that might be important, bring it out, ask them about it. Help clarify and develop the meaning of what he or she is saying.

- **The Recorder.** Listen very carefully to the interview. Take notes on the entire discussion. Make lists of important words or phrases. Try to be a good listener. Be ready to report to the larger group when it reconvenes.

This process is composed of three periods of five to six minutes each. You will rotate roles as follows:

PERIOD	PERSON	ROLE
1	A	Communicator
	B	Interviewer
	C	Recorder
2	B	Communicator
	C	Interviewer
	A	Recorder
3	C	Communicator
	A	Interviewer
	B	Recorder

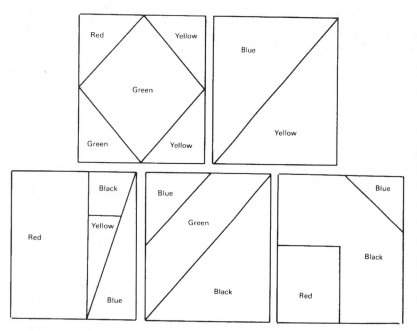

ness, pride, competitive nature, etc. Base it on the interaction of your particular group.

When each group has finished, you will have five rectangles made by piecing the colors together as shown:

To prepare envelopes, cut the above shapes from the designated colors of construction paper. Make sure they form the five rectangles. Then put all the reds in one envelope, all the blues in another, etc. These five envelopes make up enough for one group. If you have five groups, you need 25 envelopes, divided so that each of five groups can complete the puzzle and each of the five people in that group have a different color. *Larry Janse*

2. No speaking. However, you can now indicate your need for a particular puzzle piece (five to 10 minutes).

3. You may speak.

4. (optional) You may help another group finish.

This exercise usually takes 20 to 30 minutes for all the different groups to finish. The discussion follow-up must be based on the interaction during the experiment. Discussion takes place in the areas of communication and competition, drawing quickly to human feelings.

• How did you feel when you couldn't talk? Did others help you? Why was communication in your group hard or easy?

• How did you feel about the others in your group? Were they selfish or generous? Do you consider yourself generous or selfish?

• How did you feel when your group finished? Were you proud? When did you start competing with other groups? (This always happens, but never use the word team or competition. Always use groups and experiment.)

• How did you feel when another group wanted to help you? Did you like the other groups helping or did you feel like they were showing off? Which was the best group? The worst group? Why?

• How did you feel about yourself, your motives? How do you feel about your ability to communicate? the ability of people in general to communicate?

You could end up in a discussion of God's communication to people, why it is so difficult, and why he had to become a man to communicate! Or you could end up in other directions—man's selfish-

PERSONAL ENCOUNTER

This is a good experience for young people to help them learn more about human relationships. Have everyone sit in two rows of chairs facing toward each other, positioned in the following manner:

Side A X X X X X X X X X
Side B X X X X _ X X X X

There should be one empty chair. If you have an even number of participants, then the leader should participate so there will be one chair vacant. After everyone is seated, give the following instructions to the group:

• When the leader gives the signal, everyone move one chair to the right.

• After you have moved, you will have one minute to have the following interaction with the person in the facing chair:

(Person on Side A) "Right now while talking to you, I feel…(finish the sentence)."

(Person on Side B) "Why?"

(Person on Side A) "Because…(finish the sentence)."

(Person on Side B) "What can I do that would improve our relationship as members of the Christian family?"

(Person on Side A) (Respond to above question.)

After the group has reached the starting position (their original chairs), meet together for a group discussion period. The following questions can be raised:

- How did you feel talking to different people?
- How did you feel talking to an empty chair?
- Were there certain people you didn't want to talk to? Why?
- Were there certain people you wanted to talk to but didn't get the chance? (You will notice that because of the way of rotating there will be opportunity to talk to some more than once and others not at all. Youths usually catch this.)
- Was it hard to express your feeling to certain people?

A common response to this experience is fear on the part of some to talk with others in the group. This can be channeled into a discussion on the love of God and how it casts away fear. Some appropriate Scriptures would be 1 John 2:5 and 4:18. *Gary Casady*

PIGEON

Select a "pigeon" from the group and have the teen leave the room. The leader then explains to the group that they are to request of the pigeon that she accomplish a simple task without the benefit of verbal communication. The task can be anything reasonable, such as sitting in a chair and taking off one shoe, or lifting a Coke bottle above one's head.

The pigeon returns to the room and stands in the center of a circle where the group is seated on the floor. The pigeon is told that she is to accomplish a simple task in the shortest time possible. Now the group is instructed to clap (briskly) when the pigeon moves in a desired direction. For example: Suppose that the pigeon is instructed to take off her shoe. When the pigeon experiments (that is moves to the left, right, forward, backward, etc.) she should receive no reinforcement, no clapping from the group. Eventually she will experiment with sitting down, standing, etc. When she begins to sit, the group will clap briskly. When she touches her shoe (which will occur eventually), the clapping will intensify. In a matter of two or three minutes, the pigeon will remove her shoe. Remember undesired responses receive no clapping.

This is a fascinating experiment which vividly illustrates B. F. Skinner's notion of positive reinforcement and behavior modification. This is

an excellent kickoff to a discussion regarding manipulation. *Robert Lively*

LINES OF COMMUNICATION

The following exercise is designed to help young people to visualize and evaluate lines of communication and relationships between themselves and others in the youth group or the church community. In so doing, the body of Christ is strengthened as decisions are made regarding weak areas that need correction.

Divide the group into smaller groups of from four to eight persons. Each group should have a leader who has been prepared for this exercise. Each person is given an envelope containing pieces of construction paper cut into various shapes, a 14- by 22-inch piece of construction paper, and a pencil. Glue should be provided also.

The leader explains that the pieces of construction paper in their envelopes are to represent the people in the youth group (or the whole church). Each person first chooses the shape or combination of shapes that he or she feels best represents himself or herself. Be creative and honest. Each person should write their own name on this shape.

The large piece of paper represents the group (or church) as a whole. Each person should place the pieces of paper chosen to represent himself where he sees himself in relation to the rest of the group. (For example, in the center of things, on the sidelines, etc.) Next, each person should choose shapes of paper that they consider best represent the other people in the group or church and designate these by writing names on them. Then they should be placed on the blank sheet in such a way that their position represents their relationship to you. Glue them all down.

Finally, draw the lines of communication that exist between you and the others using the following types of lines:

———————— Regular real communication
– – – – – – – – Occasional real communication
〰〰〰〰〰 Talk but little communication
.... Communication through another person

(show by the route of the dots which person the communication passes through)

Other types of lines can be added for other

types of communication or noncommunication.

Wrap up the exercise by allowing the participants to share voluntarily and explain their sheet to the rest of the small group. Each person should be encouraged also to share which relationships they feel should be changed or communications improved, and how they propose to do this.

• **Friends.** Here's a spin-off from Lines of Communication. It is best with larger groups, although it will work with smaller groups, too. You will need some construction paper, scissors, paste, and something to write with for everybody. There are five steps.

1. Break into six groups (four to six people each). Each group gets different colors of construction paper and scissors. Each person cuts out eight different sizes and shapes of paper (triangles, squares, sawtooth edges, etc.) in various colors. Encourage them to be creative.

2. Have a trading round. People trade shapes with each other according to the instructions below which correspond with their birthdates. If your birthday is in:

January or February: collect shapes that are all the same color
March or April: collect four large and four small shapes
May or June: collect only shapes with one straight edge
July or August: collect only shapes with one round edge
September or October: collect at least four different colors
November or December: collect only three different colors

Shapes are traded one for one. Set a time limit and when the time limit is over, the trading is over whether or not a person has been successful at getting the right shapes, colors, etc.

3. Now explain that the various shapes of paper represent people. Each person should pick out one shape to represent himself and the other seven to represent friends they have. Names can be written on the shapes. All the shapes are then pasted onto a larger sheet of paper, with the shapes placed in a position which represents (as closely as possible) the relationships between the people represented by the shapes. Give each person a star to place on the person (shape) who is considered to be best friend. Then each person draws lines of communication between the shapes to show how well these people communicate with each other. Lines to use:

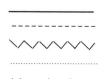
—————— Regular real communication
------------ Occasional real communication
∿∿∿∿∿ Talk but little communication
·················· Communication through another person
(show by the route of the dots which person the communication passes through)

Other types of lines can be added for other types of communication (or noncommunication).

4. After sharing with each other their finished sheets (this can be voluntary), have each group brainstorm a list of "qualities of friendship." They could write the list out with a marker on newsprint and post the lists around the room so that everyone could walk around and look at them.

5. On the backs of their sheets, have each person complete the statement, "If Jesus were on my paper (if he were a shape), my relationship would be..."

The last two steps could be deleted or revised according to your needs. The entire exercise is designed to be a springboard to thought and discussion on the subject of relationships and friends and can also be tied in with reflection on one's relationship to Christ. *Phil Beaudoin and Milton Hom*

VERBAL PUZZLE

This game can be very effective to illustrate the difficulty of following and understanding verbal directions...and it's fun. Before the meeting create puzzles (one for each participant—six to 12 kids) like the one shown in the diagram. Choose about three to six pairs of people and have the partners sit back to

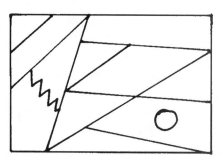

back so they cannot see each other's cut-out designs.

One of each set of partners has the puzzle-design arranged in completed order. The other diagram has the same puzzle-design scrambled. The partner with the completed puzzle describes each piece and where to place it. The pair to finish first wins. Allow all others to finish and then have a group discussion on what they learned about communication through this exercise.

Questions to ask the group members:

1. How did you feel? Confused, frustrated, angry, rushed?
2. What causes us to misunderstand what others say or mean?
3. React to this statement, "What I heard you say is not what you meant."

Don Highlander

LESSON ON LISTENING

Most of us tend to talk more than we listen. The following exercise is designed to help your kids become aware of how easy it is to miss the messages of others.

To begin, copy the four cards on page 72 and cut them apart.

Divide everyone into groups no larger than five people. Each group should be given one of the four cards. Everyone should then briefly answer the questions on the card for the whole group. After about five minutes the groups should exchange cards so that they have a new set of questions. As before, group members should take turns answering them.

After all of the groups have been through every category of questions, each person is given a sheet of paper and is asked to list every fact they can remember from the answers given in their discussion group. Of course, those with the better memories are at a slight advantage, but those who really tuned in and listened to others in their group (rather than concentrating on their own responses) will be able to recall the most. A prize could be given for the person with the most correct recollections on their list. A discussion on the importance of listening would be a good way to wrap up this exercise. For some helpful verses take a look at Proverbs 18:2,13; 22:17; and Ecclesiastes 3:7.

Lew Worthington

HUMAN TAPE RECORDER

Here is a good way to open a discussion or lesson on the theme of listening.

Have the kids pair off. One person is designated the talker; the other, the human tape recorder. On the signal to begin, the talker talks for three minutes about himself or herself. You can give talkers a list of questions or complete-the-sentence phrases to choose from, such as "When I graduate from high school, I plan to—" or "When I'm alone, I enjoy—"

When the three minutes are up, the human tape recorder "rewinds the tape"—i.e., his or her memory—and tries to repeat exactly what the talker said, in the talker's own words.

Each pair participates one at a time so that the rest of the group can judge on a scale of 1 to 10 how well the human tape recorder listened and remembered what was said. This exercise will generate a lot of laughs as well as some pretty intense listening. Follow up with your lesson or discussion.

David Washburn

DEATH AND DYING

TAKING YOUR LIFE FOR GRANITE

Many youth groups have found that visiting cemeteries is an excellent way to open up good discussion on the subject of death. A good way to follow up such an experience is to give each student a "headstone" (page 73) and instruct him to (on one side) write his name and what might appear on the headstone if he were to die today. On the other side, have him write his name and what he think might appear on the headstone should he die of old age, say 70 years from now. This allows young people to examine their lives so far, as well as their goals for the future.

IF YOU WERE TO DIE

The following exercises and questions can be used all at once or separately to discuss the subject of

LESSON ON LISTENING

Your Favorites	Exposing Weaknesses
1. What do you like most about school?	1. What is one of your weaknesses?
2. What is your favorite time of year?	2. What is your most annoying habit?
3. What is your favorite Bible verse?	3. What is your greatest spiritual weakness?
The Worst	**Revealing Strengths**
1. What irritates you the most about school?	1. What is your most positive trait?
2. What is your least favorite vegetable?	2. What is your greatest skill?
3. When was the last time you felt depressed and what do you think caused it?	3. What is your best spiritual strength?

Your Favorites	Exposing Weaknesses
1. What do you like most about school?	1. What is one of your weaknesses?
2. What is your favorite time of year?	2. What is your most annoying habit?
3. What is your favorite Bible verse?	3. What is your greatest spiritual weakness?
The Worst	**Revealing Strengths**
1. What irritates you the most about school?	1. What is your most positive trait?
2. What is your least favorite vegetable?	2. What is your greatest skill?
3. When was the last time you felt depressed and what do you think caused it?	3. What is your best spiritual strength?

Your Favorites	Exposing Weaknesses
1. What do you like most about school?	1. What is one of your weaknesses?
2. What is your favorite time of year?	2. What is your most annoying habit?
3. What is your favorite Bible verse?	3. What is your greatest spiritual weakness?
The Worst	**Revealing Strengths**
1. What irritates you the most about school?	1. What is your most positive trait?
2. What is your least favorite vegetable?	2. What is your greatest skill?
3. When was the last time you felt depressed and what do you think caused it?	3. What is your best spiritual strength?

Taking Your Life for Granite

death and dying:

1. In your opinion what is the least desirable way to die?

2. If you were to die at 11:00 p.m. tonight, who would you want most to see before you die? Choose two:

Parents	Sister	The coach
Brother	Grandparents	A child
A teacher	A friend	Enemy
A neighbor	Your pastor	

Discuss your answers and reasons why you answered the way you did.

3. Read the following scenario to your students. The handout is on page 75.

You are riding in a car down the street and all of a sudden another car that is making a left turn cuts in front of you and smashes right into your car. Your car hits the car in the lane next to you and ends up hitting a light pole. Quickly you are rushed to the hospital in an ambulance where they find out you have a fractured skull, several broken ribs, a cracked collarbone, a broken arm, and a broken leg. Needless to say, you are in bad shape and your condition gets worse every day. You fear that you will soon die. Since you have no will, you decide to write one. Write down some of your personal possessions and who you would leave them to on the handout you will receive.

Take some time to discuss the students' feelings about writing their wills and why they chose to leave certain items with certain people.

As the weeks go by your condition gets worse. Many things are tried to help you recover—special treatment, surgery by specialists—but all are to no avail, and finally you pass away. As is customary when someone dies, an obituary appears in the newspaper. Spend several minutes writing your own obituary and thinking about what will be said after you die.

You may want to read an obituary from a newspaper so the students get the idea. The form is on page 76. Take some time to review and talk over feelings about writing their own obituaries and what students think will be said about them after their deaths. *Stephen Christopher*

THOUGHTS ABOUT DYING

Read to your group the poignant true story in the newspaper article reproduced on page 77. It can stimulate your youths to discuss some of the finer, often overlooked feelings concerning death, especially sudden death. Ask the group: "If you were in this man's place, what would you write and to whom?" Or instead of using it as a discussion starter, you can simply read it at the end of a meeting before everyone leaves, as a source of private reflection. It will plant the seeds for some serious thought. *Chuck Behrens*

LIFE LETTERS

Following a discussion of suicide, have kids write a life letter to a potential suicide victim, which expresses their reasons for their belief that life is worth living. After about 20 minutes of writing, have the kids share their letters with the rest of the group (if they want to). This gives some people a chance to share their faith and provide a unique learning experience as well. *Dave Wilkinson*

FACTS ABOUT SUICIDE

To introduce a discussion about teenage suicide, give a true/false quiz (similar to the one below) to your group. Have each person write "T" or "F" on a numbered sheet of paper (1-7) after you read each statement aloud. When you read aloud the right answers afterward, ask for a show of hands of those who responded correctly. Statistics change with the passing of time, so you might want to check the accuracy of those given here or add other true-false statements as you have information.

1. People who repeatedly talk about killing themselves probably will never actually do it.
2. Anyone who tries to kill himself or herself is basically crazy.
3. If a person is suicidal, he or she will always be suicidal throughout life.
4. It is best to talk openly with someone who is suicidal about suicide rather than avoiding the subject.
5. More American teens commit suicide today than they did 20 years ago.
6. Most teenage suicides occur away from home.

My Will

I _____ being of sound mind do hereby bequeath my following possessions to the persons named below.

To _____ I leave my _____

To _____ I leave my _____

To _____ I leave my _____

To _____ I leave my _____

To _____ I leave my _____

To _____ I leave my _____

To _____ I leave my _____

To _____ I leave my _____

To _____ I leave my _____

To _____ I leave my _____

To _____ I leave my _____

Obituary For _____

_____

_____

_____

_____

_____

_____

_____

_____

_____

_____

_____

_____

'Goodbye...Be good to each other'
JAL crash victim's diary

By Jack Burton
Special for USA TODAY

TOKYO—A Japanese executive scrawled his final thoughts across seven pages of a pocket calendar in the last terrifying minutes of life aboard the doomed Japan Air Lines jumbo jet.

"I'm very sad, but I'm sure I won't make it," scribbled Hirotsugu Kawaguchi, 52. The notes were shown Sunday on Japanese TV.

As others donned life jackets, Kawaguchi wrote to his wife and three children: "Be good to each other and work hard. Help your mother."

To his son, Tsuyoshi, he wrote, "I'm counting on you."

To his wife, Keiko: "Goodbye. Please take good care of the children. To think our dinner last night was the last.

"The plane is rolling around and descending rapidly."

His 17th and last sentence was: "I am grateful for the truly happy life I have enjoyed up to now."

Kawaguchi was among 520 killed when the jet hit a mountain, the worst single-plane disaster ever.

7. Nothing can stop a suicidal person once the decision has been made.

Here are the answers to the questions above:
1. False. Most people who commit suicide give clear warnings through their words or actions.
2. False. Most teens who try to kill themselves are very unhappy or depressed, but only 15 to 30 percent are mentally ill.
3. False. If the causes of the person's unhappiness can be dealt with, he or she can probably lead a normal and full life.
4. True. This lets the person know you really care about him or her. Talking with people about suicide doesn't give them ideas.
5. True. In the last two decades, the suicide rate among American adolescents has skyrocketed to a 300 percent increase.
6. False. An average of 70 percent of adolescent suicides take place at home, between the hours of 3:00 p.m. and midnight.
7. False. Most people contemplating suicide feel a deep conflict between their desire to die and a desire to live. Intervention can change their minds.

Follow up the quiz by exploring these aspects of the subject:
• Ask if anyone in the group has ever known anyone who was thinking about suicide. (They don't have to mention names.) What did they say or do to help the person? What was the person feeling? What were they themselves feeling?
• Ask for suggestions about why someone would consider killing him or herself. Is the cause more likely to be external circumstances or an internal problem?
• If a friend talks about suicide, what do your youths think they should do? Talk to an adult about it?

With the current rate of adolescent suicide attempts so high, this is a critical topic for your kids to consider. You may even discover later that young people who have themselves thought about taking their own lives will come to talk about it with you once you've brought up the subject.

Before you conduct a program such as this, be sure to acquaint yourself with the topic by reading available resources or discussing the subject with knowledgeable counselors. If you yourself are not experienced in the area of adolescent counseling, be sure you know of someone to whom you could refer young people who may be contemplating suicide.
David Wright

DISCIPLESHIP

PERSONAL CHECKLIST

For a night of self-examination and serious thought, have your kids go through the checklist on page 79. Ask them first to check off those things which they feel they have done, without reading any passages of Scripture. Then go back over and after reading the passages of Scripture, see which ones they can check and where they need improvement. Be careful not to use this to make kids feel inadequate or guilty. Emphasize that God loves us and can still use us in spite of our failures to live in Christian perfection. You might want to close this meeting with a challenge that as Christians, if society is going to improve and change, it is we who will be changing it as Christ's servants. *Daniel Unrath*

COST OF DISCIPLESHIP

On page 80 you will find references to five New Testament Scripture passages that deal with the meaning of discipleship. The questions under each passage are excellent discussion starters to help your group focus on the main issue of each passage.

Pass out a copy of the questions and have students circle what they consider to be the best answer for each question. Each question has a place to write an answer if they feel none of the others is sufficient. *Phillip Ladd*

PERSONALITY CONTROL

Here's a discussion starter that focuses on what a Christian personality is like. Read and discuss each Scripture with the group, and have students decide how they can develop these personality traits in themselves.

• **1 Thessalonians 5:16,18:** Don't be discouraged; rejoice!
• **Ephesians 4:26:** Learn to control your anger.

Personal Checklist

_____My relationship to God is my first priority!
(Matthew 13:44-46, 16:24-27, Luke 9:57-62, 14:25-33)

_____I love others as I love myself.
(Matthew 22:34-40, Luke 6:27-36, John 14:15-17)

_____I use my talents for God's kingdom.
(Matthew 25:14-30)

_____I play the role of the servant.
(Matthew 20:20-28, 23:1-12, Mark 10:13-16, Luke 14: 7-11, John 13:1-20)

_____I help those in need.
(Matthew 25:31-46, Luke 10:29-37)

_____I do not give in to lust, even in my mind.
(Matthew 5:3, 27-30)

_____I go the extra mile asked.
(Matthew 5:38-48)

_____I always tell the truth.
(Matthew 5:21-26)

_____I am not angry with my brother.
(Matthew 5:21-26)

_____I do not worry.
(Matthew 6:25-34)

_____I do not seek security in material things.
(Matthew 6:19-21, Luke 12:13-21)

_____I forgive those who wrong me.
(Matthew 6:7-15, 1 Corinthians 13)

_____I am not judgmental in my attitude toward others.
(Matthew 7:1-5, 1 Corinthians 13)

_____I have complete faith that God will answer my prayers.
(Matthew 7:7-12, Luke 11:1-13, 18:1-8, John 14:12-14)

_____I am learning to overcome temptation.
(Matthew 18:7-9, John 8:31-38)

_____I give generously of my means.
(Mark 12:41-44)

_____I believe God will redeem his creation through Christ.
(John 3:16-17, 1Timothy 2:5-6, 1 John 2:2)

THE COST OF DISCIPLESHIP

Read Luke 9:23-25

1. To me *taking up my cross daily* means
   a. Doing things I hate to do.
   b. Facing death.
   c. Being teased because I am a Christian.
   d. Accepting anything that God desires of me as part of his plan for my life.
   e. None of the above.
   f. _____

2. Denying self means denying anything that would prevent complete commitment to Christ. For me this has meant
   a. Nothing as I haven't made this type of commitment yet.
   b. Nothing as I don't understand how to do this.
   c. Attempting to quit being lazy in my job, at home, at school, at work, or at church.
   d. To quit trying so hard and let Christ take over.
   e. Giving up my favorite TV show on Thursday to come to youth group meeting.
   f. _____

Read John 17:13-24

1. Being *one* here means
   a. Doing things together.
   b. Never disagreeing. Always accepting the other's viewpoint.
   c. Learning to love, share, and work closely with each other.
   d. _____

2. This oneness can be achieved by
   a. Denying self—and sharing our gut feelings with each other.
   b. No longer disagreeing with others.
   c. Getting to know others in the group better.
   d. _____

Read 1 John 3:23, 24 and John 13:34-35.

1. This type of love means
   a. Action—I must share myself with others.
   b. Attitude—finding the good in other people.
   c. Love others enough to help them with their problems.
   d. All the above.
   e. _____

2. A *personal relationship with God* to me
   a. Is asking Christ to forgive me.
   b. Is having visions of God talking to me.
   c. Is something that won't really happen till heaven.
   d. Means accepting Christ as my best friend.
   e. _____

Read 1 Corinthians 15:49 and 1 John 3:2

1. Becoming like Christ means
   a. Sinning less and less.
   b. Learning to love as Christ loved.
   c. Learning to minister for Christ better.
   d. Growing in knowledge of God and the Bible.
   e. _____

- **James 4:6:** Don't be conceited; be humble.
- **Ephesians 5:14:** Don't be lazy; wake up!
- **Matthew 20:25-27:** Don't be pushy; serve others.
- **Colossians 3:15:** Don't be restless; be content.
- **Ephesians 4:32:** Don't be rough; be tender.
- **2 Corinthians 1:3-4:** Don't pity yourself; comfort others.
- **Ephesians 5:21:** Don't be stubborn; submit.
- **1 Thessalonians 4:11-12:** Learn to be quiet and mind your own business.

Steve Fortosis

SAFECRACKER

For kids to demonstrate for themselves the risk that is part of faith, try this: before arriving at the youth meeting, fill a safe or combination lockbox with a handful or two of candy—as well as with 10 dollars, or with something similar that's valuable to your students (and something you don't mind giving away).

Then distribute the note on page 82.

After the consultations and loans and safecracking and paybacks, discuss how following Jesus requires risk-taking—putting yourself out on a limb, burning your bridges behind you, setting yourself up for seeming failure. Cite examples of risk takers in Scripture, such as Abraham, Noah, Moses, Jeremiah, Paul. *Mike McKay*

INDIVIDUAL TAX RETURN FOR GOD'S GIFTS

This fake Form 1040, see page 83, is a discussion starter about using time and talents for the kingdom of God. It takes a while to fill out, and it works better with older teens than it does with junior highers. Since the person "filing the return" has to carry information to various other places on the form, different people can have different results. *David R. Holmes*

DIVORCE

DIVORCE PANEL

Here's a program that can help your kids develop a more realistic picture of the effects of divorce than they usually get from TV or the movies. It can also help them know how to help a friend whose parents are divorced or divorcing. Finally, it can be used to support kids whose parents are already divorced.

First, ask several kids whose parents are divorced to serve on your panel of experts. Give them a list of potential questions in advance to help them decide whether or not they can handle the experience, and allow them to decline if they'd rather not be on the panel.

The adult who moderates the panel should be carefully chosen—someone who is sensitive to the pain which most of these kids experience. The moderator should do some pertinent reading ahead of time on the effects of divorce on children. A number of articles have appeared on the subject in both Christian and secular publications.

Here are some sample questions for the panel:

- How did you find out about your parents' decision to divorce? Did the way in which you were told help or hinder your acceptance of the divorce?
- What kinds of feelings did you (or do you) have about the divorce?
- Did your role in the family change after the divorce? How?
- What kinds of things did friends do or say in response to the divorce? What do you wish they had done or said?

This can be a powerful and instructive program for both the audience and the panel. *David Wright and Al Arcuni*

DRINKING

THE BALLOON TRIBE

Sometimes the best way to approach a topic is to come in through the back door. The allegory on page 86 opens up a good discussion of drinking and substance abuse in a non-threatening way.

After the group has read or heard the story of the Balloon Tribe, divide up into three groups according to the position each student takes toward the story:

SAFECRACKER

Before you is a treasure you'll enjoy—believe me. Simply be the first one to open the lock, and it's yours. Here's the combination: 21-9-____. The last number? Oh, yes, If you want the last number, you'll need to give

_____
Sponsor

_____
Amount

And one other thing—no teaming up. If you want the last number to the combination, you must pay up individually. You can borrow from others if you want, but only if you pay them back within one week.

SAFECRACKER

Before you is a treasure you'll enjoy—believe me. Simply be the first one to open the lock, and it's yours. Here's the combination: 21-9-____. The last number? Oh, yes, If you want the last number, you'll need to give

_____
Sponsor

_____
Amount

And one other thing—no teaming up. If you want the last number to the combination, you must pay up individually. You can borrow from others if you want, but only if you pay them back within one week.

SAFECRACKER

Before you is a treasure you'll enjoy—believe me. Simply be the first one to open the lock, and it's yours. Here's the combination: 21-9-____. The last number? Oh, yes, If you want the last number, you'll need to give

_____
Sponsor

_____
Amount

And one other thing—no teaming up. If you want the last number to the combination, you must pay up individually. You can borrow from others if you want, but only if you pay them back within one week.

SAFECRACKER

Before you is a treasure you'll enjoy—believe me. Simply be the first one to open the lock, and it's yours. Here's the combination: 21-9-____. The last number? Oh, yes, If you want the last number, you'll need to give

_____
Sponsor

_____
Amount

And one other thing—no teaming up. If you want the last number to the combination, you must pay up individually. You can borrow from others if you want, but only if you pay them back within one week.

1040G   **Individual Tax Return for God's Gifts**   19____

LABEL

Your first name and initial   Last name

_____

Home address

_____

City, State, and Zip

_____

FILING STATUS

1. ☐ Christian

2. ☐ Nominal Christian

3. ☐ Non-Christian

4. ☐ Nominal Christian filing as Christian, hoping no one knows

5. ☐ List name of person you think you are fooling _____

EXEMPTIONS

If your time value in this section is less than once per week, please use an appropriate fraction to represent the value of time for one week.

List use of your talents for God.

Total the number of times the talent is used per week.

Event
Example: Use of vocal talent by singing in choir.   2

6. _____   _____

7. _____   _____

8. _____   _____

9. _____   _____

10.   Total . . . . Enter here and on line 30.

Total time per week.

List use of your time for God.

If a line is blank, please enter zero (-0-) on the appropriate line.

Event
Example: Reading Bible daily for 30 min. each day.   3.5 hrs.

11. _____   _____

12. _____   _____

13. _____   _____

14. _____   _____

15.   Total . . . . Enter here and on line 35.

Total amount per year.

List use of your money for God. (Do not include the tithe.)

Event
Example: Money given to Christmas Missions Offering. $50

16. _____   _____

17. _____   _____

18. _____   _____

19. _____   _____

20.   Total . . . . Enter here and on line 44.

INCOME

For talents include all possibilities: musical ability, helpfulness to a friend, ability to visit the sick, to visit shut-ins, to witness, etc.

21. Enter total number of talents you possess. .... _____

    x7

22. .... _____

    x52 [ ]

23. Enter total number of hours God gives you per week. (If this is something other than 168, attach an explanation.) .... _____

    x52

24. .... [ ]

25. Enter total monies available to you from all sources. _____
26.   Multiply line 25 by 10% _____
27.   Subtract line 26 from line 25. .... [ ]

TAX COMPUTA-TION

28. Enter amount from line 22 .... _____

    x10%

29. This is the number of talents God expects you to use.. _____
30. Enter amount from line 10 .... _____

    x52

31. This is the number of talents used for God ..... _____
32. Subtract line 31 from 29. This is the number of talents owed God .... [ ]

33. Enter amount from line 24 .... _____

    x10%

34. This is the amount of time God expect.......... _____
35. Enter the amount from line 15 .... _____

    x52

36. This is the amount of time given to God .... _____
37. Subtract line 36 from line 34. This is the amount of time owed God .... [ ]

38. Enter the amount from line 26 .... _____
39. Enter the amount you have given toward your tithe._____
40. Subtract line 39 from line 38. This is the amount owed for tithe .... [ ]

41. Enter the amount from line 27 .... _____
42. Enter the percentage of your money you feel God wants you to give as an offering to him ... _____%
43. Multiply line 41 by the percentage on line 42 ... _____
44. Enter the amount from line 20 .... _____
45. Subtract line 44 from line 43. This is amount due God in offering................................. [ ]

OTHER TAXES AND PENALTIES

46. If you have ever sinned, please check this box. ☐ (See instructions in Romans 3:23.)

47. If you checked the box on line 46, then your penalty is hell for eternity. (See instructions in Romans 10:9, 10.) List your penalty here...... ─────────

CREDITS

a. If you checked box 1, then your penalty has already been paid by Jesus Christ. You qualify for a reward in heaven. Write "heaven" on line 48.

b. If you checked box 3, then you must eventually pay the amount on line 47. You may change your status to box 1 if you work out details with Jesus Christ. If you do not work out such details, then enter on line 48 the information from line 47.

c. If you checked box 2, then your penalty has already been paid by Jesus Christ—though you may not understand or appreciate the fact. (See the New Testament for details.)

d. If you checked box 4, Jesus Christ will audit your return. He knows the truth anyway—and he can set you free (see b. above).

48.. ☐

TOTALS AND PAYMENT

Enter the amount from line 32......... ☐ Due in Talent
Enter the amount from line 37......... ☐ Due in Time
Enter the amount from line 40......... ☐ Due for Tithe
Enter the amount from line 45......... ☐ Due for Offering

PLEASE MAKE ARRANGEMENTS TO FULFILL THESE REQUIREMENTS IN THE NEAR FUTURE. FAILURE TO DO SO WILL RESULT IN THE LOSS OF VALUABLE BLESSINGS THAT ARE ALREADY AVAILABLE FOR YOU. ADVANCE AND EXCESS PAYMENTS WILL BRING YOU THE BENEFIT OF ADDITIONAL BLESSINGS.

Enter the information from line 48 _____

IF THIS IS ANYTHING OTHER THAN "HEAVEN," THEN THE INFORMATION ON BLESSINGS AVAILABLE DOES NOT APPLY TO YOU. WE ENCOURAGE YOU TO CONSIDER FILING STATUS NUMBER ONE. IT DOES REQUIRE SACRIFICE ON YOUR PART, BUT IT ALSO COMES WITH A FULLY FUNDED RETIREMENT PLAN THAT IS TRULY OUT OF THIS WORLD.

For more information please see Romans 3:23; 6:23; 10:9,10,13.

Signed: _____

The Balloon Tribe

There is a tribe in a primitive country across the ocean with a unique social activity. This is the story of how that activity originated and the effect it had on the tribe. It seems that a short while back, one of the tribe members discovered a stretchy substance which came from a local tree. With limited experimentation at first, the tribe didn't think this discovery was very important. However, from that substance one tribe member was able to invent what we know as a balloon. The tribe thought it a clever but seemingly useless invention.

One day, however, that same tribe member discovered something interesting about the balloons. After blowing up several of them, he became light-headed and out of breath, experiencing a euphoric dizzy feeling. When he told of this to the rest of the tribe, everyone immediately wanted to try it. Eventually, as this activity increased, the tribe became divided into four groups: The "Dizzy Balloon Blowers," the "Occasional Balloon Blowers," the "Balloon Blowers for Career or Craft," and the "Anti-Balloon Blowers."

The Dizzy Balloon Blowers developed a tolerance to blow up several very large balloons in just a short time—usually in just one evening. This group would get together every week and blow up numerous balloons for many different reasons: Some would do it to get dizzier than the time before; some as just a reason to get together with their friends; some because it was a way to relax after a hard day in the jungle; some to celebrate; and others just because they weren't getting along with other tribe members. Each tribe member felt that his or her reason for blowing up balloons was worth it, even though they often felt sick and nauseated in the morning, promising never to blow up another balloon.

Now the Occasional Balloon Blowers enjoyed a balloon every once in a while. In fact, when they did join the Dizzy group, they would take up a whole evening just blowing up one balloon (which was usually not too large). These tribe members blew up balloons for all the same reasons as the Dizzy group, but were careful to avoid having to go through what the Dizzys went through the morning after.

The Balloon Blowers for Career or Craft turned balloon blowing into an art. They only blew up the best balloons, not just any old cheap balloon. In fact, many of this group made their own balloons. And fine balloons they were! It was not long after balloons were discovered that this group started contests and competitions to find the "best." They examined balloon shape, size, color, and how well it expanded. Many in this group got very good at making balloons and did so full-time.

On the other side of the jungle were the Anti-Balloon Blowers. They had seen the damage done from blowing up too many balloons and getting dizzy. They loudly protested that absolutely no one should blow up balloons! Some members of this group had in the past been Dizzys. Balloon blowing had caused tribe families to break up and hate one another, they said. Many tribe members had given up their tribal responsibilities so they could blow up balloons all day and get dizzy. Some Dizzys got too dizzy even to paddle their canoes home, and so they drowned trying to do so.

With the many groups of balloon blowers—and the Anti-Balloon Blowers—it was difficult to assess the overall benefit or detriment to the tribe as a direct result of the balloons. Some members would not touch balloons while some seemingly could not face life without them. In some way every tribe member had to make up his or her own mind.

- Blowing up balloons is fine and it's okay to run out of breath and get dizzy if you feel like it.
- Occasional balloon blowing is okay, but it's morally wrong to get dizzy.
- Blowing up balloons is wrong at all times.

Have the groups defend their positions and allow switches if desired. *Larry A. Dunn*

EMOTIONS

ANGER

Here's a powerful way to interest your group in a session on anger. First recruit one young person beforehand to play the role of photographer. From the beginning of the meeting time, the photographer shoots flash pictures of the games, singing, and announcements. You then gently ask him to please stop taking pictures and repeat this with increasing intensity as he continues to go ahead and take more pictures anyway.

As the serious time of the meeting approaches, you give the photographer one last ultimatum. Then just as you start to speak, he takes one last picture. You react with fury, walk over to the young person, grab the camera and pull out the film, shouting about the previous warnings. The kids will react in a variety of ways, and the atmosphere will be highly charged. The situation turns around when you walk back to the front and say, "Tonight we are going to discuss handling our emotions. Let's start with anger." Debrief the episode by pointing out the tremendous power of one angry person and the various reactions of the group to the anger that you demonstrated.

Possible questions for discussion:

- What makes you angry?
- What do you do when you get angry?
- How do you deal with anger?
- Anger is listed as one of the seven deadly sins. Is anger a sin? Or is it a normal human emotion?
- What does the Bible teach about anger?
- Do Christians express anger differently from non-Christians?

David C. Wright

JESUS HAD FEELINGS, TOO

The purpose of this activity is to help kids realize the humanness of Jesus Christ. The focus of the program is on emotions.

For this activity you need pencils, paper, felt tip markers, one large sheet of poster board, a coin, and a table against a wall. During the activity a game board is constructed and used. If time is short, the game board can be created in advance by one of the group leaders.

First, introduce the subject of emotions, noting that we all have them, and that they are normal and part of being human. Emphasize that it's how we respond to and express our emotions that determines whether they lead to growth or problems. Next, pass out paper and pencils and ask the youths to think of their family, school, and friends. As they remember different emotions they've experienced because of these people, they should write the emotions down.

Now ask them to think of Jesus Christ and his life as we know it through the Bible, writing down a separate list of emotions they believe he experienced.

Once the lists are complete, have the youths read their two lists aloud to the other members of the group while a volunteer compiles two lists from their suggestions. (Each emotion should appear only once in each list.) If the list of feelings or emotions is shorter for Jesus than for the rest of the group, use the opportunity to talk more about Christ's humanness and perhaps add some ideas. Now transfer the complete list of emotions to the poster board as in the diagram.

Forgiveness	
Love	Fear
Compassion	
Anger	Sadness
Joy	
Amusement	Grief
Loneliness	

To use the board, place it on a table against a wall. Each person takes a turn throwing the coin at the board from a reasonable distance. Whatever emotion the coin lands on, the player must think of one situation from the Bible where Jesus could conceivably have felt that emotion. He or she must also describe how Jesus expressed it.

To personalize this game even more, you can ask players to describe an occasion when they themselves experienced that particular emotion, and how they expressed it. They should also say how they think it should have been expressed.

After everyone has had a turn, conclude the activity with a prayer asking Christ's help in expressing emotions in ways that help rather than hurt. *Sean Mahar*

ENCOURAGEMENT

APPRECIATION GAME

This is a small-group experience to be followed by a discussion. Form groups of from five to seven in each group. The groups sit in a circle with a chair in the center. One person in the group sits in the center chair with the rest of the group around him. As long as he sits in the center chair, he must remain completely silent. Each person in the circle then tells the person in the center three or four things he appreciates about him. This is done by each person one at a time. The kids are instructed to
• Be honest. Be as deep or as superficial as you like. Just don't be phony.
• Speak directly to the person in the center.
• Be specific and detailed.

This continues until everyone has been in the center chair, with everyone in the group telling what they appreciate about the person in the center.

Following this experience, have the group discuss the following questions:

• **Was it easy to receive these compliments? To give them? Why?**
• **Did you feel discomfort?**
• **Did you want to avoid communicating directly with the other person?**
• **Did you want to avoid or reject these messages of liking?**
• **Did some people in your group find it difficult to follow directions? To keep silent?**

About saying things of appreciation without

cutting down the other person? About respecting the rights of others to speak? *Robert Fisk*

ENCOURAGE ONE ANOTHER

Give everyone a piece of paper and have someone help pin it on their backs. Then ask the group to circulate and write one thing they like about each person on his piece of paper. This may take five to 15 minutes, depending upon the size of the group. Allow time for each person to read his own piece of paper. Follow with a devotional on the need to encourage each other using such passages as 1 Thessalonians 5:14 and Hebrews 10:24. *William Moore*

PASSING OUT COMPLIMENTS

Have the group sit in a circle and give out a sheet of paper and a pencil to each person. Instruct everyone to write his or her name at the top, and then pass it to the person on the right. Now have everyone write down one thing he or she appreciates about the person whose name appears at the top. Then pass the sheets to the right again and repeat the procedure. Sheets should go around the circle in this way until they reach their owners again.

Now go around the circle and ask each person three questions:

1. **Which was the funniest comment on your sheet?**
2. **Which was the most heartwarming?**
3. **Which surprised you the most?**

Next, have people voluntarily tell something they wrote on another person's paper, speaking directly to that person. When everyone who wants to has had a chance to give a compliment directly, talk about how they feel when they're openly praised this way (good, awkward, proud, embarrassed). Ask how long it's been since group members received a compliment face-to-face, and if it's been a while, talk about what keeps us from praising one another. End by reading 1 Thessalonians 5:8-15 together. *Phil Nelson*

NAME AFFIRMATION

Have each young person write his or her name vertically down the left side of a lined sheet of paper, one letter to a line. Pass the papers to the left.

Then have each person write a compliment about the person whose name is on the paper so that the compliment

J oyful
A ccepts others
Y ou like to be around him

S ecret-keeper
A ttentive
R eally listens to you
A lways helpful
H appy

begins with one of the letters in that person's name. Pass the sheets to the left again and repeat the procedure so that an acrostic of compliments is formed by each name. Letters can be used more than once if all the letters are filled.

After all the names have been filled this way, each person is introduced by the person holding his or her name, who reads the compliments aloud. Then the paper is returned to its owner. *Karen Dockrey*

PICK A COMPLIMENT

When teaching on encouragement get the ball rolling with Pick a Compliment. After copying the compliments on page 90, cut them apart and then do one of these activities:

• Pass around a hat containing the compliments. Each person pulls out a compliment and lays it on the person on his or her right. Encourage players to ham it up.

• Print each compliment on a full sheet of paper

and pass out one sheet to each person. Announce a timed contest to see who can compliment the most people in the allotted time using the written compliment. After complimenting another player the student offering the compliment gives his or her paper to the newly complimented person to sign. *Jack Hawkins*

EVANGELISM

COMMERCIAL RELIGION

There is no doubt that commercials influence every aspect of our daily lives so they can be an effective media technique. There are some dangers, however:

• Commercials tend to entertain rather than inform.

• Commercials tend to consolidate reality, simplify reality into very black and white categories.

• Commercials tend to exaggerate, manipulate.

• Commercials tend to use symbols.

There are many other dangers when it comes to commercials and it is very important that a youth group not accept commercials as valid communication devices and feel that by just changing one word, that the entire meaning will change. For example, the phrase, "Coke is it," changed to "Christ is it." True, statements like that are catchy, but the question is, is the new statement true? And in what ways is it true?

But because most people hear commercials all the time, it can be a lot of fun to allow your youth group to make some commercials for God, Christ, or the church by adapting popular commercials, or by creating entirely new ones. Divide your youth group (if possible) into small groups and give the groups a few minutes to create their own commercials around whatever theme you give them. Give the kids enough time to practice and gather together whatever props they need. Then have the groups present their ideas to each other one at a time. You might tell the group something like this: "You have been given 60 seconds (or 30 seconds) on national prime time television. Create and produce a commercial for God, Jesus, or the church. Millions of people will see it. What kind of spot would you create?" *Nancy Fravel*

Pick a Compliment

You have the greatest teeth.

Your liver holds a lot of bile.

You have really cool ears.

I like the scent of your deodorant.

You have the nicest nostrils I've ever seen.

You have the most hairs on your head per square inch that I've ever seen.

You have the prettiest pinky I've ever seen.

Your clothes have really cool pockets.

You have a great sense of smell.

You have hardly any dirt between your toes.

I really like your shoelaces.

You have great eyebrows.

You have the prettiest middle name I've ever heard.

Your fingerprint is a piece of art.

Your ears hardly build any ear wax.

You have the cleanest neck I've ever seen.

Your tongue has more taste buds than anyone else's.

You have a great intestinal tract.

I wish my stomach digested food as quickly as yours does.

TRACT DRAFT

This can be an excellent way to discuss the significance of gospel tracts and at the same time help your young people understand what the gospel is.

First bring a variety of sample gospel tracts for your kids to look over. You should make sure you have a variety of styles from hard core fundamentalism to denominational and fairly contemporary tracts. Discuss each of the tracts including questions like:

• What is the purpose of tracts?
• Is it possible for a tract to be effective? If not, why not? If so, are there any exceptions?
• If you think it is possible to have a good tract, what criteria would you use, if any?
• Have you ever been handed a tract? If so, what was your reaction? What was the reaction of other people?
• Have you ever given anyone a tract? Why? What happened?

If you as a group have come to the conclusion that tracts can be used and have developed some criteria for their use, then divide up into groups (if large enough) and write your own tracts. Encourage creativity! Let them use their imaginations. Then have the entire group evaluate each tract. *Ray Houser*

COMMUNICATION GAME

Choose a volunteer. Explain that on a piece of paper you have drawn a circle, a square, and a triangle. These three figures are all in a certain relationship to each other. This person is to look at the drawing and then describe it to the others, effectively, so that they can reproduce it correctly on paper. The figure may look like any of these:

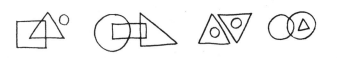

Everyone in the audience has a piece of paper and pencil and is ready to write. Then have your volunteer stand with his or her back to the audience and simply describe the figures in words.

Next, compare drawings—there will be quite a variation.

Choose another volunteer to do the same thing, only this person may face the audience and use his or her hands in describing the figures. Once again, the audience writes down what the second person has described, and then compares notes. You will find that there are still many differences.

Choose a third person to do the same thing (of course, each time the drawing is different). This time the person may face the audience, use his or her hands, and answer questions. The audience writes down the figure and checks it again with the original. This time almost everyone has the right answer.

Communication is not just words; it also involves gestures and motions—it must be personal. Communication is a two-way process. Read Acts 1:8 and discuss its implications for witnessing, then conclude with specific application and challenge.

A STICKY SITUATION

This is an object lesson that takes its central idea from 2 Timothy 2:15. Prior to the meeting, a stick of any length is prepared and bound with spirals of masking tape. Only you know the exact length (it should be whole inches, not fourths or halves). To begin the discussion you ask the group to describe the stick as to shape, size, color, texture, anything that might be a clue as to its identity. Next you ask all of them to come to where you have placed the stick on a table or chair and, without touching the stick in any way or using any known measurements, try to decide the true length of it by just looking at it. After five or 10 minutes, divide the group according to their conclusions as to the length of the stick. (For example: all who believe it to be 12 inches in one group, 14 inches in another group, etc.)

After the group is divided, you then tell them to try to convert everyone who is in another group to their group; allow 10 or 15 minutes. This will get loud and amusing; let it—that's part of the lesson. After time is up, divide them up into groups again just as before, but watch for those who have changed groups. Then start the real lesson. The leader needs to ask what some of the problems were that they encountered while trying to convert others to their way of thinking. Usually someone says that they didn't know the length of the stick because it couldn't be measured, so they couldn't really convert people. Then ask the ones who changed groups why they changed. You can ask the ones who were certain of the length why they were so positive. The results are interesting and serve as a springboard to launch your group into gaining more knowledge of their own Christian witness. Wait until your discussion is completely over before revealing the true length of the stick. *Bill Bellah*

THE GREAT FISH CONTROVERSY

The parable on page 93 is excellent for stimulating discussion on evangelism and the ministry of the church. (Written by Ben Patterson. Reprinted from *The Wittenburg Door* by permission.)

REAL EXPRESSIONS OF FAITH

The point of this exercise is to help the group express its faith without using Christian clichés that non-Christians may not understand. Give each person a paper bag, each with a different food item: carrots, bananas, marshmallows, onions, Twinkies, candy, cookies, oranges, apples. Participants must attempt to persuade the rest of the group to attend a banquet where the food in their bag will be the main course. The hitch is that they can't name the food explicitly, describe its taste or smell, or compare it to other foods. The kinds of words they can use are ones like these:

soft	shallow	funny
hard	aristocratic	impulsive
firm	pleasant	flat
elegant	light	puffy
common	tough	bright
uplifting	proud	interesting

The group then votes on the food they want to have for a banquet. The person who does the best selling job should receive some kind of prize (a blue ribbon, or maybe a gift certificate to an ice cream parlor).

Follow this activity with a discussion of some common Christian clichés used to describe God, the church, or our faith. Work toward redefin-ing these clichés in terms of fresh language or metaphors, or even street language. Add to the following list of clichés any others you may want to discuss: the body of Christ; Savior; Lord; saved by the blood; born again; covered with the blood; blessing; I feel in my spirit. *Erlan and Jan Leitz*

ALIEN

Have most of your group grown up in the church? Alien forces them to express what Christianity is all about—without using Christianese.

Arrange for an adult who has some acting ability and can think on his feet to be an alien. He needs to be a stranger to the kids, familiar with evangelical lingo (saved, born again, washed in the blood, etc.), and creatively able to push the kids to define God, Bible, sin, etc., when the words or ideas are used.

Dress the alien as outlandishly or subtly as you want, and fabricate a story line: Swhnoztall arrived recently from the Mizar System in order to study terrestrial culture. He's having trouble, however, with religion—for his own planet's culture is without a deity, and consequently he has neither a word nor even a concept of one. He is visiting your youth group because he heard that they could help clarify for him what Earth religion is.

The alien essentially controls the discussion, forcing your students to explain without the familiar terms what Christianity is. The kids will struggle through defining why they believe God exists, why he loves them, how to follow this God, what a personal relationship with him is like, the incarnation of Jesus, etc. The alien should guide the conversation to the fact that Jehovah is God of the universe—including the Mizar System—and wants to be Swhnoztall's God, too, so that he can take home with him the good news of the Man-God.

Don't end without pointing out that their high school friends may be as clueless to Christianese as Swhnoztall is and that they must explain the Gospel in terms unbelievers can comprehend. *Mary Gillett*

THE GREAT FISH CONTROVERSY

For months, the Fishers' Society had been wracked with dissension. They had built a new meeting hall which they called their Aquarium and had even called a world-renowned Fisherman's Manual scholar to lecture them on the art of fishing. But still no fish were caught.

Several times each week they would gather in their ornate Aquarium Hall, recite portions of the Fisherman's Manual, and then listen to their scholar exposit the intricacies and mysteries of the Manual. The meeting would usually end with the scholar dramatically casting his net into the large tank in the center of the hall and the members rushing excitedly to its edges to see if any fish would bite. None ever did, of course, since there were no fish in the tank.

Which brings up the reason for the controversy. Why?

The temperature of the tank was carefully regulated to be just right for ocean perch. Indeed, oceanography experts had been consulted to make the environment of the tank nearly indistinguishable from the ocean. But still no fish.

Some blamed it on poor attendance at the Society's meetings. Others were convinced that specialization was the answer: perhaps several smaller tanks geared especially for different fish age groups.

There was even division over which was more important: casting or providing optimum tank conditions.

Eventually a solution was reached. A few members of the Society were commissioned to become professional fishermen and were sent to live a few blocks away on the edge of the sea and do nothing but catch fish. It was a lonely existence because most other members of the Society were terrified of the ocean. So the professionals would send back pictures of themselves holding some of their catches and letters describing the joys and tribulations of real live fishing. And periodically they would return to Aquarium Hall to show slides.

After such meetings, people of the Society would return to their homes thankful that their hall had not been built in vain.

DON'T TALK WITH YOUR MOUTH FULL

In most of our affluent churches, discussion on food and fasting can be very worthwhile with youth. Such a discussion can be wrapped around a study of biblical fasts to determine the relevance or need for fasting today. A few quotations are on page 95 that might be helpful to stimulate interest in the topic. Here are some questions to get you going:

• How do you react to Finney's statement? Why?
• What do you think Finney meant when he used the phrase "the appetite for food"?
• How could Finney link the idea of "powerlessness in the church" with the appetite for food? Do you think it is valid?
• How is it possible to eat to the glory of God?
• How much gluttony does it take to make one gluttonous?
• What is your definition of fasting?
• Is fasting a valid form of worship for people today? Why?

FISHERS OF MEN

Kids can learn that sharing their faith needs to be as specialized as the fishing styles and equipment of avid anglers.

Find some professional or sports fishermen in your congregation or among your young people's families. Ask to borrow some of the specialized gear

they use to go after different fish—different kinds of tied flies, wading boots, a deep-sea fishing pole, a more common rod and reel, a simple cane and can of worms, a casting net—even a piece of the rope used in nets of professional deep-sea fishermen. If some of the owners of the equipment are willing, invite them to come to the meeting to model their

own gear and explain why fishermen need such equipment in order to catch the particular kind of fish they want to hook (or net). If you haven't got any takers, dress up several of the kids in either borrowed or makeshift gear.

Introduce each fisherman or each style of fishing, describe the equipment on display, and explain (or ask the fisherman to explain) the method used to catch the desired kind of fish. Ask the fishermen to demonstrate their techniques.

Then explain that, in their attempt to catch fish, fishermen change their approaches according to the kind of fish they want. The goal of Christians is to be fishers of men. Our choice of equipment and methods must reflect the needs and background of the individuals we approach. Sometimes a simple, straight-forward approach will do the job—like the cane and the can of worms. Some fish respond only to refined bait that flicks their attention your way long enough to give the message. Sometimes you must wear thigh-high boots to wade in to meet people where they are. Those under the influence of deeply addicting sins require heavy-duty equipment to counter their intense resistance to the gospel—but they, too, need to know and experience the love of Jesus.

Russ Porter

PICTURING FORGIVENESS

Have the kids look up the following Bible passages and list from them as many "word pictures" about

HE HAS REMOVED MY SIN AS FAR AS THE EAST IS FROM THE WEST — PSALM 103: 11-12

how God forgives our sins as possible. Most kids ought to be able to come up with five or six. The passages are: Isaiah 38:17, Isaiah 43:25, Psalm

DON'T TALK WITH YOUR MOUTH FULL

"Food is not the most basic essential in life. The greatest bodily need is Air. The second is not food, but Water. Third is not food, but Sleep! Food comes fourth but in thousands of Christians' lives, it seems to be put first. Too much food clogs the system. To over-eat is a sin of waste and a sin against the body, shortening the physical life and dulling the spiritual. If you are not its master, you are its slave!" —*Winkie Pratney*

"The appetite for food is perhaps more frequently than any other the cause for backsliding and powerlessness in the church today. God's command is 'whether you eat or drink, or whatsoever you do, do all to the glory of God.' Christians forget this and eat and drink to please themselves. They consult their appetites instead of the laws of life and health. More persons are snared by their tables than the church is aware of. A great many people who avoid alcohol altogether will drink tea and coffee that in both quality and quantity violate every law of life and health. Show me a gluttonous professor and I will show you a backslider." —*Charles Finney*

"It is important for us to distinguish between a desire or appetite for food and a hunger for food. It is doubtful whether the average individual, reared in our well-fed Western civilization, knows much of genuine hunger. The sensation of emptiness or weakness, gnawing in the pit of the stomach, and other symptoms experienced at the outset of a fast are seldom real hunger. They are a craving for food resulting from the long-continued habit of feeding ourselves three times a day without intermission for three hundred and sixty-five days a year." —*Arthur Wallis*

103:11-12, and Micah 7:18-19. These word pictures might include someone being pulled from a well, throwing sins behind your back, blotting out or wiping away sins (off a blackboard perhaps), and so on.

After the kids have done this, have them choose the one which seems to be most meaningful to them personally. Give them some markers and paper or other art supplies, and have them actually draw, paint, make a collage, or use any other method to present graphically their forgiveness word picture. When the pictures are completed, allow kids to share the meaning of their pictures with the rest of the group.

Finally, spend about five minutes with the entire group brainstorming a completely unique word picture for forgiveness, not one found in Scripture. You might want to make it very contemporary or it could be very abstract. This can also be graphically pictured, perhaps as a large mural to hang on the wall of the meeting room or elsewhere in the church. *Robert Nordlie*

FRIENDSHIP

FRIENDSHIP DISCUSSION

Friendships are of primary importance to most young people. Some good questions for an effective discussion of friendship are on page 97. For best results, print them up for distribution and have the kids answer each question on their own before discussing them with the entire group. *Bill Curry*

FRIENDSHIP SKITS

Next time your group discusses friendship, start with this idea. Brainstorm with your group to list all the qualities of a good friendship. Then search for Scriptures that comment on or complement your list (for example, Proverbs 18:24, Ephesians 4:31-32, Colossians 3:12-15).

As the group is compiling this list, have someone write down the traits on 3x5 index cards, one trait per card. When the listing is finished, divide the kids into groups of about five, have each group pull three cards from the friendship-traits card deck, and then give them five to 10 minutes to create a skit or mime that demonstrates their three qualities. During performances, the audience tries to guess what traits are being described.

Follow up with a discussion about practicing those qualities that make strong friendships. *Bob Stebe and Lucy Bernhardt*

SAM SMILEY'S USER-FRIENDLY FRIENDSHIP CHARACTERISTIC CATALOG

This lesson encourages students to think about the characteristics they value in friends. Introduce the lesson by reading or dramatizing the following:

You have just entered the Twilight Zone, and you're in a quandary. The darkness around you is fearful. You have this strange feeling of extreme loneliness. You find you are in a placid, sterile, hospital-like room all by yourself when suddenly you feel a startling tap on your shoulder. You spin around.

There in front of you is a vertically challenged salesman with a big smile. He immediately places his hand out and says, "Hi. My name is Sam Smiley the Salesman. I'm in the business of selling friends and from the looks of you—you seem very friendless to me." Sam Smiley's wrist watch alarm starts beeping obnoxiously. As he glances at his watch, he exclaims, "Oh no! I'm late!"

He reaches into his pocket and hands you his catalog of friendship characteristics. He starts to run off, but before going more than a few feet he stops and says, "I forgot. Here's a free gift certificate that you can use to buy anything from my catalog worth up to $25.

Give each student a $25 gift certificate (page 98) and a copy of "Sam Smiley's User-Friendly Friendship Characteristic Catalog" (page 99) which contains descriptions of 22 friendship characteristics and their costs. Teens create an ideal friend by redeeming the gift certificate for as many

FRIENDSHIP

1. **What is friendship? How do you define it?**

2. **Why do we need friends?**

3. **Describe a perfect friendship.**

4. **Describe a lousy friendship.**

5. **Name some of the qualities of a successful friendship you can learn from the following verses:**

   1 Samuel 18:1; 19:1-7; 23:16-18   Mark 2:1-4   Proverbs 17:17
   Proverbs 27:5-6   Job 2:11-13   Ecclesiastes 4:9-11

6. **In what ways is God a very special friend? (See the following verses for ideas.)**

   Hebrews 13:5-8   1 Peter 5:7
   Romans 8:38-39   John 15:13

7. **Fill in this box for your three closest friends:**

Friends' names	Why he or she is my friend	What my friend contributes	What I contribute	How our friendship could improve
1.				
2.				
3.				

Sam Smiley's

USER-FRIENDLY FRIENDSHIP CHARACTERISTIC CATALOG

SERVING THE GREATER METROPOLITAN AREA WITH FRIENDLY FRIENDS
PLEASE ENCLOSE YOUR $25 GIFT CERTIFICATE. ORDERS OVER $25 NOT ACCEPTED.

$4 Athletic Can play football, volleyball, basketball, soccer, baseball, field hockey, swim, wrestle, run, jump, vault—you name it. Extra fee charged for sumo wrestling and rugby.

$3 Reliable Guaranteed to be on time and to do what he or she says.

$5 Has a sense of humor Creates lots of laughs. Has graduated from the Lotsa Laughs School of Humor. Scored low on the Sarcastic Survey as well as the Biting Humor Test.

$3 Popular Guaranteed to have a multitude of associates and friends available at all times.

$5 Has a car Has 24-hour access to a car of his or her own. Guaranteed not to be older than 10 years, and guaranteed not to be a station wagon.

$3 Has similar interests Compatible with six or more of your primary activities. Does not collect stamps or go to antique stores.

$3 Considerate This model goes the extra mile. Does not step on your toes.

$2 Kind Included with this positive characteristic are trustworthiness and encouragement.

$4 Intelligent Average I.Q. of 135. Capable of holding high-ranking positions. Bonus: this model likes to help you with homework.

$5 Sincere Always tells you the truth and reveals how he or she feels.

$3 Christian Card-carrying, full-fledged, born-again believer in Jesus Christ.

$5 Honest Completely truthful in all situations. Guaranteed never to stab you in the back.

$2 Same age Guaranteed to have been born within one year of your birthday; this model promises compatibility.

$2 Good-looking Graduated from the VaVaVoom Beauty School, with honors. You'll look better just standing next to this person.

$4 Wealthy Just recently inherited a large sum of money from a rich but dead uncle. Bonus: does not mind sharing.

$2 Lives nearby Within a mile of your house, in fact.

$3 Has a pleasant personality Always happy and content with life.

$3 Has no other friends Desperate for someone just like you to be his or her best friend.

$4 Good listener Always willing to lend a listening ear or a shoulder to cry on.

$5 Fun Knows how to have a good time.

$2 Has nice parents Comes as a set. Will not embarrass you under any circumstances.

$3 Does not gossip Does not have a mouth that tells everyone everything. Once you tell him or her a secret, you know it won't be spread throughout the county.

LIST BELOW ALL FRIENDSHIP CHARACTERISTICS YOU'D LIKE TO ORDER.

Discription: _____ _____ _____ _____ _____ _____ _____

Cost: _____ _____ _____ _____ _____ _____ _____

TOTAL: $_____

characteristics as they can afford to purchase.

Follow up by breaking into small groups to share answers. Discuss why certain qualities are preferred. Help students draw conclusions consistent with Scripture and make personal applications. *Duane Steiner*

GENDER

REAL MEN, REAL WOMEN

To start discussion about what it means to be truly masculine or truly feminine, create a list of well-known men and women. Be sure to draw from a variety of categories such as politics, sports, entertainment, and faith. Keep in mind the ages of your students. Ask each young person to rank the women from one to seven according to their femininity (one is the most feminine, seven is the least). Then have them do the same for the list of men, ranking them according to their masculinity. When your students have finished, make a tally of each personality's rankings to determine who was most rated #1 and who most often came in last. Talk about which qualities were considered in the ranking.

Next, choose a few of the following questions to continue the discussion:

• How would you define masculinity/maleness? What does it mean to be a man?
• How would you define femininity/femaleness? What does it mean to be a woman?
• Who has the right to define masculinity and femininity?
• Is it unmasculine to express emotions openly and cry in front of people?
• Is a boy who doesn't like sports unmasculine?
• Is it masculine to be macho?
• Is a girl athlete unfeminine?
• Is an aged woman unfeminine?
• Is it feminine to be a female "sex symbol?" Is it masculine to be a male "sex symbol?"
• Does physical attractiveness make a person more masculine or feminine?
• To what extent are our concepts of masculinity and femininity influenced by God? Our parents? Our peers? The media?

Conclude the discussion with some biblical references on the subject: Psalm 8; Genesis 1:27, 31; 2:18-25; Galatians 3:26-29. *Jim Olia*

MALE AND FEMALE

Find out what God has to say about the whole issue of men's and women's roles. Begin by giving each person a copy of the questionnaire on page 101.

Discuss student answers. Then have someone read Genesis 1:27-28, 2:18-25, Galatians 3:25-29, and Philippians 2:1-8.

Follow up with these questions:

• Why do you think God made the different sexes?
• What do you think God's attitude toward men and women was then (and is now)?
• What are some of the benefits of the differences between the sexes?
• Having read the passages in Galatians and Philippians, how should we as Christians view the sexes? Is one superior to the other? How do they complement each other? How should we treat each other as a result?

Conclude by having the group think of some specific things they could do to help understand the opposite sex better, such as learning more about the types of things the opposite sex is interested in, stopping to think the next time they are about to make a disrespectful or prejudicial comment, or becoming aware of how they may have locked themselves and others into certain roles that don't allow for the unity we have in Christ. *Anna Hobbs*

GOALS

A MODERN PARABLE

The pressure of meeting goals is the subject of this discussion starter. Read "Bill the Boll Weevil" (page 102) imaginatively (or assign a student to practice then deliver it). Discussion questions can be found on page 103. *Doug Partin*

MALE AND FEMALE

1. What does it mean to be female? (Or what does it bring to your mind?)

2. What does it mean to be male? (Or what does it bring to your mind?)

3. Girls: I feel most feminine when...

   Guys: I feel most masculine when...

4. I think a man/woman feels most masculine/feminine when...(describe how you think the opposite sex feels).

5. List a few personality differences between men and women.

A Modern Parable
BILL THE BOLL WEEVIL

Way back when, there was a Bolivian boll weevil named Bill. Like other beetles, Bill was badgered by his parents about becoming better. So instead of being content living life one boll at a time, Bill set a goal of becoming the most famous boll weevil in all of Bolivia.

When Bill told his friends, they scoffed at his goal and told him to quit being such a Bolshevik. Well, Bill bolstered his belittled ambitions and decided to take a bold step. He determined to become the strongest boll weevil in all of Bolivia. Sure, he thought, that would make him the most famous boll weevil of all.

So while his bourgeois friends bloated themselves and basked under blistering beams and balmy Bolivian breezes, Bill was burning calories and building brawn. At first he could barely bench a discarded boll, and he had to learn how to breathe from his belly. As time passed, however, he became buff enough to heft basketballs and eventually bowling balls.

When Bill began bragging about his strength, his friends laughed at "Barrel Chested" Bill's bunch of balderdash. So Bill bet a bunch of bolls that he could bench the ball, and before a bewildered bunch of beetles, he performed the feat. As he bulked up, his fame broadened throughout all Bolivia. Beetles from around-about came to see Bill the boll weevil bench balls, bassoons, even boulders.

One day the bigwig of Bolivia, taking advantage of Bill's popularity, invited Bill to a command performance. Billboards announced the event, and ESPN was on hand to cover the sensation. Proud boll weevils wore B-shirts that billed Bill as the best boll weevil in all of Bolivia.

Excitement was in the air. The bigwig had given Bill his fill of barbecued bolls. Bill donned a bright bolero with matching bolo and bolted over to the Baldwin baby grand. Amid the oohs, aahs, and ballyhoos, Bill hefted the Baldwin up and balanced it on one finger. The crowd went wild. Bill was just beginning to bow when he let loose a gut-bursting belch. He bobbled the Baldwin, and it came down with a bang, leaving bashed Bill with broken bones and a badly bruised ego.

A Modern Parable
BILL THE BOLL WEAVIL DISCUSSION QUESTIONS

1 Who do you know who lives like Bill? Do you live like Bill?

2 Because of what people you respect tell you, your lives may be filled with demanding goals that you feel are important. For example, you've all heard these famous last words:

- You have to spend time studying to make good grades.

- You have to make good grades if you plan to go to college.

- You have to go to college if you want a good job.

- You have to get a good job if you want to live the good life (afford a spouse, house, kids, cars, vacations, etc.).

- You have to be a good steward if you want to retire comfortably.

3 Imposed goals can make a life heavy, burdened, unenjoyable. They can even destroy a life by instilling the lie that no matter what you achieve, it is not enough. So you exhaust yourself trying to achieve goals someone else instilled in you—until you collapse under the pressure. It's not that the goals are evil—only that there's more to life than the goals may allow.

4 True or false? Explain your answers.

- One's goals inevitably affect one's attitudes.

- Materialistic preoccupation is a necessary evil today.

- The expectations of others often spur you on to a better quality of life.

- Peer pressure usually pulls you down.

- The cost of success—that is, of reaching goals—is usually worth it.

5 Let's read Matthew 6:25-34. (Ask some students to paraphrase it.) Consider these questions:

- What should be your primary goal (or goals) in life?

- Who imposes this goal?

- What kind of life can you expect if you strive for this goal?

- Why pray about reaching goals—whether about grades, jobs, etc.—when you could worry about them instead?

- How much time do you spend worrying about reaching a goal? How much time do you spend praying about reaching a goal?

- What should God's care for his creation teach you?

- Will God take care of your physical needs if you don't work?

- Will God take care of your physical needs if you work on seeking his kingdom and his righteousness? How do you expect this to be done?

- If you took this Scripture seriously, how would it affect your life today?

SPIRIT BALLOONS

Here's a unique idea that can be used for planning meetings or for group discussions on goal-setting for the future. Since this idea involves the role of the Holy Spirit, begin by defining the word *spirit*. It is used in the Old and New Testaments and means "breath" or "wind." With this short definition in mind, have students write down a long-term goal that they have, a career they would like to pursue, or anything that involves dreaming big about things to come.

Fold the papers on which the dreams have been written and put one inside each uninflated balloon—one balloon per person. As students inflate the balloons, remind them of the definition of *spirit*—they are surrounding their dreams symbolically with the Holy Spirit. Discuss how all of our dreams and goals are made possible by the Holy Spirit and how dependent we are upon him.

Tie all of the balloons and place them in the middle of the room. Using a game or random selection, pop some of the balloons, read the goals aloud, and discuss what is necessary in order for a person to accomplish that goal. *Mark Christian*

LIFE GOALS

Here's a good discussion starter about setting goals in life. Distribute the handout on page 105 and have the kids rate the life goals (for their own lives).

When they've finished, have the kids look up the following Scripture passages and determine what they have to say about setting goals:

> Psalms 27:4
> 1 Kings 3:5-13
> Exodus 33:18-23
> Phillipians 3:7-10

Next, have the kids list their top three goals, along with a few good ways to achieve them. *Steve Fortosis*

GOSSIP

GOSSIP GAME

The Scriptures have a great deal to say about the consequences of idle gossip or murdering with the tongue. The following game is useful as a way of pointing out the futility of spreading rumors.

Choose three young people to leave the room while a fourth person copies (as best she can) on poster board a picture that she is shown.

One of the three persons outside comes in and draws the same drawing only using the first person's drawing as his guide, rather than the original.

The next person comes in and draws her drawing from the second person's, and likewise with the last person.

The last person's drawing is then compared with the original and, of course, there will hardly be any resemblance to the original at all, since each of the young people copied each other, and everyone changes their drawing a little, usually omitting or adding important things.

This object lesson is entertaining as well as revealing, and can be followed up with a discussion on gossip using Matthew 18:15-17 as a wrap-up. *Steven Dyk*

HONESTY

TO TELL THE TRUTH

This is a great program idea for an entire meeting that is highly entertaining as well as extremely productive. The meeting is based on the old TV game show, "To Tell the Truth."

Before your meeting begins, find a kid who has done something unusual or humorous that no one else in your meeting knows about. For example, the teen may have gotten lost at Disneyland as a kid, won a soap-box derby, or gotten sick on a jet plane to Europe—anything that nobody else would know about. Then get two other impostors who will pretend that they did the same thing. With the

Life Goals

Rate the following:

	Got to have it	Would be nice	Not neces-sarily for me
To have a great family without any hassles			
To have all the money I want			
Never to be sick or seriously injured			
To find a good-looking and fulfilling mate			
To do what I want when I want			
To have the power the President has			
To be the best-looking person			
To have a great hunger for the Bible and prayer			
To be able to understand all things			
To eliminate all hunger and disease in the world			
To be always super-close to God			
Never to feel lonely or put-down			
To know the future			
To be able to learn quickly and excel in all things			
To be filled with God's presence in the most dynamic way			
To know always that I'm in God's will			
To be the greatest athlete in the world			
To become a famous movie star			
To always have a lot of close friends who never let me down			

help of the mystery person, write out an affidavit similar to the type used on the TV show, which should describe the unusual event. The affidavit should be as humorous as possible.

To open the meeting, the three kids come out, state their real names, and tell what they did. For example, the first guy might say, "My name is John Schmo and I got lost at Disneyland." The second player says, "My name is Rita Klutz and I got lost at Disneyland," and the third player does likewise. Then you read the affidavit describing what happened when the mystery person got lost at Disneyland.

The three kids are seated at the front and the audience (one at a time) asks them questions to try to figure out who did it. For example, somebody might ask, "Number one, how old were you when you got lost?" and so forth. After about 10 minutes of questions, the audience gets to vote for who they think did it. A show of hands for each of the three players is the best way to vote. Ask various people why they voted for each particular teen. After the show of hands for each of the three kids, you ask, "Will the real person who got lost at Disneyland please stand up?" And the real teen does. This concludes the first part of the meeting, which should be carried out as casually and with as much fun as possible.

After the game, a discussion should be held on the subject of honesty. Listed below are some sample questions for discussion:

• What is dishonesty?
• When is dishonesty justifiable? (Give examples)
• Is there such a thing as a white lie?
• What is the most dishonest thing that a person could do?
• How can you determine a lie from the truth?
• Give an example of dishonesty in our society; in business; in religion; in government.

Encourage the group members to be honest as they discuss these questions and perhaps to share personal experiences when they have been dishonest and what the result of that dishonesty was.

CLUE

Prearrange to have several games of Clue brought to your weekly meeting. The day before your meeting,

contact several teenagers and tell them they are to cheat as much as possible in the game (have one cheater for each game). After the game explain what has been done. Discuss the following:

• Ask what kinds of feelings they had toward those who were dishonest.
• Ask the cheaters how they were treated by the others.
• Discuss whether the group considered it to be normal for there to be cheaters in the game.
• Discuss the biblical view of honesty.

Paul Cox

THE SCIENCE TEST

The topic of cheating is always relevant for young people, since cheating on exams and homework is almost accepted behavior on many campuses. The following situation requires kids to face a tough decision and to respond as they think they might if the situation were real.

As you walk into your biology class, you notice a lot of tension in the air. Everyone knows that the teacher is planning on giving a difficult test to the class the next day. As you sit down at your desk, you notice a sheet of paper laying on the radiator next to you and you inadvertently glance at it. You realize that you are looking at the master copy for tomorrow's test. Before you know it you have carefully read down the whole page. Your friend sitting behind you notices that you are mesmerized by the piece of paper on the radiator and, out of curiosity, looks over at it. Before long a small crowd has gathered around the test and around your desk. Everyone is rapidly soaking up the questions; some students are even writing the questions down. Everyone scatters when the teacher enters the room, but it's too late; the teacher already noticed the crowd and approaches the paper. The teacher picks up the paper and realizes that it is the master copy he has misplaced. He looks at you and says, "This is tomorrow's test. Do you know if anyone looked at it?" You feel as if the eyes of the world are upon you. How will you respond?

Discuss these questions:
• How will you respond? What are your options?
• What could be the outcome of each option?
• What are some of the motivations behind each option?
• Why would it be so hard to do the right thing?
• What is at stake in each option?

• What do the optional responses reveal about a person's values?

As you wrap up the discussion, try to give kids some positive help and guidance rather than condemnation and/or moralizing. *Jim Walton*

FENDER BENDER

Read this dilemma that can open discussion about shades of truth. By the way, this episode really happened.

For a few months now you've been looking for and praying for a new electric guitar. You figure that you play well enough to warrant the investment. One Saturday morning your mom asks you if you want to go with her to check out the garage sales. Your first stop is the weed-infested yard of a small, shabby house, in front of which sits an elderly woman. As your mom browses for odds and ends, your eye catches a dusty guitar and amplifier sitting just inside the garage. You know guitars enough to know that this guitar-amp pair lists for around $1300; you've seen them go for half that, used, in the classifieds. You have only dreamed of owning a guitar and amp like these.

You swallow hard before speaking to the woman, and try to sound casual. "How much are you asking for that guitar and amp over there?"

"Oh, I don't suppose it's worth much," she mutters. "It doesn't even have any strings on it anymore. It belonged to my son before he died in a swimming accident last year. You can have them both for $35. Are they worth that much to you?"

What do you do?
1. Reason that it is her responsibility to know the value of her merchandise; say, "Yes, I think they're worth that much to me. I'll take them;" pay her $35 for them; and thank the Lord for answered prayer.
2. Explain to her the market value of the guitar and amp.
3. Talk her down to $30. *Jon Adam*

CHRISTIAN BUDDY MACHINE

Have a guy dressed up like a robot with a sign on him that says CHRISTIAN BUDDY MACHINE 10

CENTS. A lonely man waiting for a subway tells the machine his problems, deposits 10 cents, and the Buddy Machine gives him all the usual Christian pat answers to his problems. This can lead to a good discussion of the church or Christians who know what to say but who lack real personal love and concern. *Sheldon White*

LOVE

ENTERTAINING ANGELS UNAWARES

Begin your class as usual, but plan to have an interval where the kids will be free to move about and talk for about five or six minutes. While class is starting, have a really obnoxious looking person come in and take a seat in the back (he will be a friend of yours incognito, of course). While the move is going on, have this person try to approach some of the kids (he can be loud, drunk, very shy, paranoid, etc.). Just before the five to six minute period is over, he will leave. When everyone is situated again, read a relevant passage of Scripture (1 Corinthians 13:4-8, John 13:34-35, Matthew 22:34-40) and explain the strange person. Have him come back in and the class can then discuss their reaction to him, how he felt, how Jesus would have reacted, and the mission of the church in reaching the socially outcast. *Steven E. Robinson*

GIFT GUESSING

This activity allows kids to give to each other, to share with each other, and to have fun all at the same time. To begin, make up some cards like the one shown here so that everyone's name is on a card.

Mix up the cards, place them in a hat or bag, and let each kid draw one (make sure kids don't draw their own names). Then kids should write FROM and their own name on their cards below the name already on the card. At the bottom of the card they should identify a gift they want to give to the named person—preferably an intangible gift such as "good health for the rest of your life." Gifts should be creative, thoughtful, and suitable for each recipient.

Next, have kids tear the cards in half, putting the name half in their pockets and the gift half tacked to a large bulletin board. Kids must then choose the gift they think was chosen specifically

for them, remove it, and try to find the person who gave it to them. If they are wrong about the gift, they can try to find the correct gift and trade with whoever has it. By a process of elimination, everybody eventually will come up with the right gift and giver. At first there will be a lot of chaos and laughs but the results are rewarding.

Close by discussing all that went on during the activity—how you felt about the gift that was given to you, the gifts that were given to others, and so on. *Julia Thompson*

HOW LOVE IS EXPRESSED

This is a program designed to explore the ways that Christian love is expressed in different relationships. The method is role-play and discussion. Divide into groups and assign each group a situation to role-play. The groups are specifically instructed to express Christian love in the situation they are portraying. Each group will present its role-play and follow it up by asking the question, "How was Christian love expressed?" Everyone lists the ways and also includes ways that were possibilities, but were not acted out. Analyze the list created. Discuss the different types of love, possibly bringing to light the biblical distinction between *agape*, *eros*, and *phileo*.

Here are three suggested situations. The number of characters and their sexes can be adjusted to fit your group.
1. *Characters*: mother, father, John, Mary.

John and Mary return to Mary's home to tell her parents that they have become engaged.

They have gone together for a year and a half and are both in their 20s. John will graduate from college in May.
2. *Characters*: pastor, three youths, the old lady.

A pastor takes three church youths to visit an elderly lady. She lives alone in a rundown house.
3. *Characters*: a husband and wife, an agnostic friend.

The husband and wife are devout Christians. An old agnostic college roommate is visiting them. Conversation turns to religion and the friend expresses hostility toward the church. He says, "The church is full of hypocrites."
Donald Musser

LOVE IS

A simple way to get kids involved in an object lesson on the subject of love is to hang a large sheet of poster board on the wall in the shape of a heart. Written on the heart are the words LOVE IS... If hung up several weeks in advance, kids will write their definitions all over the heart. Some will be frivolous, but some will be worth discussing. *Leonard Phelps*

PARAPHRASING THE LOVE CHAPTER

Here is a way to allow kids the opportunity to put some of their own thought into the Love Chapter of the Bible, 1 Corinthians 13. Leave key words or phrases out of the verse, but leave enough in that the basic idea will still be communicated. Have the kids then fill in the blanks with whatever they think fits best for them. Afterward compare student

1 Corinthians 13
If I have all the ability to talk about_____, but have no love, then I am nothing but a big _____. If I have all the power to _____, but have no love, then my life is _____. If I understand everything about _____, but have no love, then I might as _____. If I give away _____, but have no love, then I _____. Love is patient, love is kind, love is _____. Love never _____.

versions with the the original. Let students read their completed versions to the entire group. By doing an exercise such as this (it can be done with other portions of Scripture as well), kids are forced to think through the meaning and application of the passage. *George Gaffga*

LYING

FALSE WITNESS

Ask one of the prominent members of the church to prepare a sermon of about 10 minutes in length. The person should be someone the youths see quite often, but don't actually know very well. And the sermon should be full of half-truths and basically be theologically incorrect. It should be subtle, though, so as not to appear a blatant lie.

As the sermon is being presented, see how long it takes your group to disagree with what is being said. In one group where this was done, the man who gave this sermon used Scripture references, taken completely out of context, and finished without any of the youths challenging him. After the sermon, we went back over what he had said, and they pointed out things they had disagreed with. When asked why they didn't say so before, the most common reply was, "Because he is an adult, a good Christian, and we figured he knew what he was talking about."

Use this as a springboard for a discussion about false teachers and how we determine what the truth really is. Some Scripture references to use: 2 Corinthians 11:14-15, 1 John 4:1-6, 2 Peter 2:1-2, Matthew 24:4-5, 11, 24-25, Jude 4. *Pam Bates*

OBEDIENCE

MEDITATING DAY AND NIGHT

Starting off with the mind-blowing idea that people actually loved to meditate on the Old Testament law day and night (see Psalm 1:2 and Psalm 119 in

its mammoth entirety), have your kids pick two of the Ten Commandments (each individual makes a personal choice), isolate themselves, and meditate on them for five to 10 minutes. Tell them that nothing much happens in meditation for the first five minutes, so be patient. After they've had some time to get quiet, introduce a couple of questions for them to think about:

- What kind of world it be if everyone obeyed this commandment?
- What kind of world would it be if nobody obeyed it?

Following the meditation period, have the kids share some of their thoughts relating to the specific commandments they chose. The following discussion questions can be used:

- Which commandments did you choose and why?
- How would you answer the previous two questions (What kind of world...)?
- Why do you think biblical commands are resisted so much today?
- Do Christians still have to obey Old Testament laws?
- Are laws necessary in the church?
- Which laws are hard for you to obey?

Dave Phillips

PEER PRESSURE

INFLUENCE SURVEY

The survey on page 110 will get kids thinking about influences on their lives. *Joe Harvey*

PRIORITIES

TIME GAME

A hands-on object lesson in evaluating priorities, this game asks kids to fit their activities into specified periods of time in a diagram. Following the exercise, discuss making choices about how to spend time.

Add several local and seasonal activities—

INFLUENCE SURVEY

Rate each of the following according to the degree of influence they have on your thinking and behavior. Place an "X" in the category that applies.

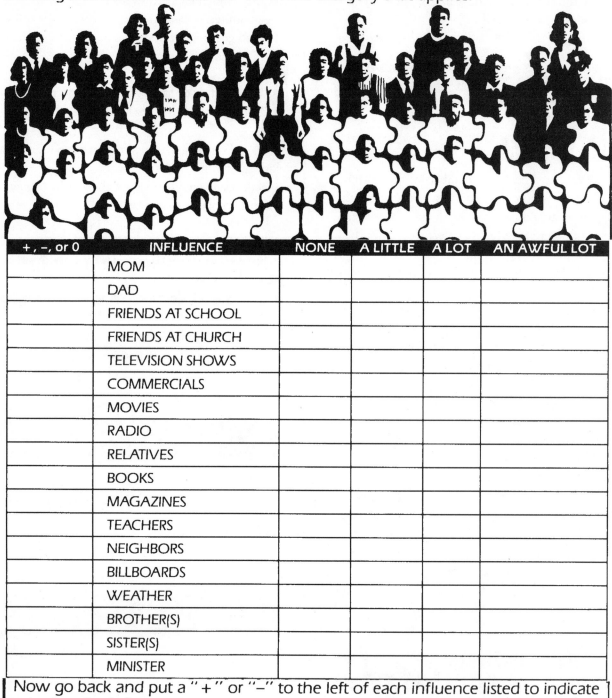

+, −, or 0	INFLUENCE	NONE	A LITTLE	A LOT	AN AWFUL LOT
	MOM				
	DAD				
	FRIENDS AT SCHOOL				
	FRIENDS AT CHURCH				
	TELEVISION SHOWS				
	COMMERCIALS				
	MOVIES				
	RADIO				
	RELATIVES				
	BOOKS				
	MAGAZINES				
	TEACHERS				
	NEIGHBORS				
	BILLBOARDS				
	WEATHER				
	BROTHER(S)				
	SISTER(S)				
	MINISTER				

Now go back and put a " + " or "−" to the left of each influence listed to indicate whether the influence is mostly positive (+) or negative (−). If you think the influence is neither positive or negative, put a "0" by the word.

football, finals, Christmas shopping—to the hand-out on page 112. Make copies and distribute it along with the handout on page 113. Have your students cut out the paper strips of activities. Then they place whichever strips they want—and can fit—into the allowable space. Activity strips may not overlap.

When the students finish, ask questions like these to kick off discussion and reflection:

• Do your choices reflect how you actually spend your time?
• Which activities did you leave out?
• How did you choose which ones to eliminate?
• How do you feel about the activities you left out?
• Why did you include certain activities?
• Did you choose activities out of obligation or genuine desire to include them?
• Do your choices of activities have anything to do with your long-term goals?
• How does your relationship with God affect which activities you included?
• Is Jesus' example of spending time helpful? (Mark 1:35-39 is one example of how Jesus managed his time.)
• How, if at all, has this discussion caused you to rethink your choices?

Tim Gerarden

PRIORITIES

Open the eyes of your kids to their values with this activity.

First, the preparation:

1. Make an envelope full of priorities for each student, like this: Copy the Priorities sheet provided on page 114 (one per student) and choose 10 words or so from the list that you think appeal most to your group's students. Cut out those 10 words (slips)—plus the two slips that say JESUS CHRIST and LIFE ITSELF. Put each sheet's 12 slips into an envelope; when you're finished, you should have as many envelopes as you'll have kids in the meeting.

2. Now make another set of envelopes: Cut out the verses at the bottom of each sheet along the dotted lines. (Depending on your youth group, the tone of the meeting, and your doctrinal views, you may or may not want to include the second verse on each slip. It's up to you.) Put each slip by itself in an unmarked, sealed envelope. But keep track of which slips are in which envelopes; there should be a subtle way for only you and a trusted volunteer to identify which slip, A or B, is in each envelope. Give these two sets of envelopes to that volunteer to hold until later in the game.

3. Prepare a list of Bible trivia questions—from your previous Bible studies, from the game Bible Trivia, etc.

Now for the game:

Hand each student an envelope of priorities, a sheet of paper (to record answers to the trivia questions), and a pencil. Explain to them that in each envelope are a variety of things that are probably important to them. For each trivia question they answer incorrectly, they must forfeit one of their priorities out of their envelope—except the two priorities JESUS CHRIST and LIFE ITSELF, which are fundamental to everything else.

Now ask the Bible trivia questions. After each question students write their response, then you give the answer. Kids with correct answers do nothing; kids with incorrect answers forfeit one of their priority slips. Make the trivia questions difficult enough so that most kids are reduced to only two priority slips before long JESUS CHRIST and LIFE ITSELF.

Here's where your volunteer gets busy. When students who are trimmed down to those two priorities answer another trivia question incorrectly, they have a choice to make: they sacrifice to your volunteer one or the other of their final two priorities. Your volunteer notes which one is handed to her—and gives the student in exchange one of her envelopes.

A player who turns in the JESUS CHRIST priority (by implication valuing life itself above Jesus Christ) receives from the volunteer the sealed envelope containing slip A ("What good will it be for a man if he gains the whole world, yet forfeits his soul?"). A player who turns in the priority LIFE ITSELF (by implication valuing Christ over physical life) gets a sealed envelope containing slip B ("Whoever finds his life will lose it, and whoever loses his life for my sake will find it").

Don't allow the students to open their envelopes until everyone has finished playing. Then separate the students into two or more groups according to which envelopes they received (or by grade in school, or by gender, etc.), and ask them to

TIME GAME

ACTIVITIES

TV

school

part-time job

school club / sports

dating

movies

video games

washing dishes

brushing teeth

housework

church

prayer

homework

hanging out with friends

talking on the phone

TIME GAME

YOUR DAY

Cut apart the Activities slips on the
other sheet, then choose the ones
you want to fill your day—This box.
No overlaping!

PRIORITIES

Life Itself	American Rights	Family
Jesus Christ	Reputation	Girl / Boyfriend
Music	Travel	New Clothes
Popularity	Well-fed	Best Friend
Telephone	Fame	Job
House	Leisure	Neighborhood
Sports	Comfort	Pets
Parties	Money	Pride
Car	Good Health	Stereo
Parents	Success	

Slip A

What good will it be for a man if he gains the whole world, yet forfeits his soul?
(Matthew 16:26)
Depart from me, you who are cursed, into the eternal fire prepared for the devil and his angels.
(Matthew 25:41)

Slip B

Whoever finds his life will lose it, and whoever loses his life for my sake will find it.
(Matthew 10:39)
Welcome, you who are blessed by my Father; take your inheritance, the kingdom prepared for you since the creation of the world.
(Matthew 25:34)

open their envelopes. This should lead to a great discussion on priorities.

For an extended game include more than 12 priorities in the students' envelopes. *Michael Shipman*

RUN FOR YOUR LIFE

Although this strategy deals with the subject of death, it is really about life and how we live it. The purpose of this exercise is to help young people to evaluate their priorities in light of what is really important. It allows the group members to contrast what they are doing now with what they would do it they only had one month to live. Give each person a copy of the handout on page 116.

Ask your students to evaluate the items by marking how likely they would be to do or not do the activity described (definitely yes to absolutely not) on the continuum. Then have them rank the activities from first to last choice. The first item on the list is the one the student would be very likely to do and the last is the one the student would be very unlikely to do.

Have students share their choices, explain why they chose that way, and then discuss the results with the entire group. *John Boller, Jr.*

PRIORITY SLIPS

Reproduce page 117, one copy for each student. Cut the slips apart and place one set of 12 in each envelope. Give an envelope to each student.

Tell the group that the phrases complete the statement, "A Christian should be..." They must study the slips, decide which four are least important, and put those four back in the envelope. From the remaining eight they must now choose the four most important. Those four must then be prioritized and numbered one through four (one is the most important).

Talk about the results when they finish. This simple exercise will help kids recognize their priorities as Christians and give you a good idea of what kinds of programming are needed for your group. *Joe Harvey*

WE ARE BRIDGE BUILDERS

Here's a good program idea dealing with the topic of reconciliation, both our being reconciled to God through Jesus Christ and being called to be reconcilers ourselves.

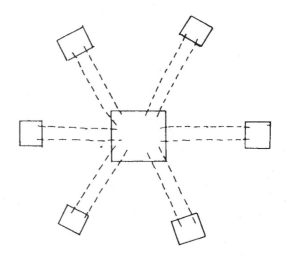

Begin with some fun games and maybe some singing, and then divide the group into bridge-building teams, with six or seven students on each team. The teams can be larger or smaller, depending on your group. Then give each team lots and lots of popsicle sticks—the more the better. They are not expensive so make sure you get enough. Also provide tape or quick-drying glue for each team.

In the center of the room place a cardboard box. Each team gets an additional smaller box which they place about four or five feet from the

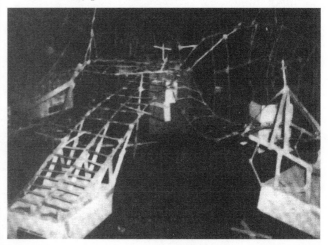

115

RUN FOR YOUR LIFE
IF I ONLY HAD ONE MONTH TO LIVE, I WOULD—

__1. Perform some high risk feat that I have always wanted to do, figuring that if I don't make it, it won't really matter.

Yes, definitely   Absolutely Not

__2. Stage an incredible robbery for a large amount of money which I would immediately give to the needy and starving of the world.

Yes, definitely   Absolutely Not

__3. Not tell anyone.

Yes, definitely   Absolutely Not

__4. Use my dilemma to present the gospel to as many people as I could.

Yes, definitely   Absolutely Not

__5. Spend all my time in prayer and Bible reading.

Yes, definitely   Absolutely Not

__6. Make my own funeral arrangements.

Yes, definitely   Absolutely Not

__7. Offer myself to science or medicine to be used for experiments that might have fatal results.

Yes, definitely   Absolutely Not

__8. Have as much fun as possible (sex, parties, booze, whatever turns me on.)

Yes, definitely   Absolutely Not

__9. Travel around the world and see as much as possible.

Yes, definitely   Absolutely Not

__10. Buy lots of stuff on credit that I've always wanted: expensive cars, fancy clothes, exotic food, etc. ("Sorry, the deceased left no forwarding address.")

Yes, definitely   Absolutely Not

__11. Spend my last month with my family or close personal friends.

Yes, definitely   Absolutely Not

__12. Not do anything much different. Just go on as always.

Yes, definitely   Absolutely Not

__13. Isolate myself from everyone, find a remote place and meditate.

Yes, definitely   Absolutely Not

__14. Write a book about my life (or last month).

Yes, definitely   Absolutely Not

__15. Sell all my possessions and give the money to my family, friends, or others who need it.

Yes, definitely   Absolutely Not

__16. Try to accomplish as many worthwhile projects as possible.

Yes, definitely   Absolutely Not

__17. _____

Yes, definitely   Absolutely Not

__18. _____

Yes, definitely   Absolutely Not

PRIORITY SLIPS

Supportive of mission projects	Supportive of mission projects
Faithful in church attendance	Faithful in church attendance
Studying the Bible to learn more about God	Studying the Bible to learn more about God
Active in community affairs	Active in community affairs
Sharing his or her faith	Sharing his or her faith
Looking for opportunities to help others	Looking for opportunities to help others
Constantly seeking God's assistance in daily life.	Constantly seeking God's assistance in daily life.
Truthful and dependable	Truthful and dependable
More concerned about others than about himself or herself	More concerned about others than about himself or herself
Modeling his or her life after Jesus' example	Modeling his or her life after Jesus' example
Angry at what's wrong in the world	Angry at what's wrong in the world
Kind and friendly to strangers	Kind and friendly to strangers

cardboard box in a circle.

Each team is then instructed to build a bridge from its box to the box in the middle, using the popsicle sticks, tape, and glue only. All the bridges would then be joined together (reconciled).

This activity can produce total participation, a lot of creativity, and plenty of laughs. Encourage any extras that youths might want to add, such as toll booths, cars, and so on. You might offer a special prize to any group whose bridge will support a toy truck or something like that. Follow the whole thing up with a discussion of the unexpected things that happened during the process. There will be many insights on "bridge building" that you just can't get any other way. *Bruce MacCullough*

SALVATION AND GRACE

HOW TO GET TO HEAVEN

Many times young people can get all bogged down with the theological terms of justification, redemption, atonement, sanctification, and so on. Here is a very effective game that helps kids understand the meaning of forgiveness, faith, and grace. Announce that the object of the game is to get enough points to get to heaven. In order to get to heaven, students must have a total of 1,000 points. Points are awarded or deducted according to things they have or have not done (see page 119).

Divide the entire group into small groups of four or five each and distribute copies of the handout. Each group has 15 minutes to see how many points they can come up with. They can combine points (within the small groups) to try to get a total of 1,000, but in that case, only one person can go to heaven for each 1,000 points accumulated. Choosing who gets to go is a good source of discussion all by itself.

For added incentive, you might offer a chocolate sundae or some other desirable award to anyone who is successful at making it to heaven.

Of course, you can make up your own lists, depending on the emphasis you would like the game to have. You can add some, subtract others, or change the value of the items. Stress the impor-

tance of honesty while kids are computing their point totals. Try to structure your point system so that the kids can at least get a few points and not end up with a minus score. This phase of the game ends by having the groups announce who (if anyone) gets to go to heaven, and perhaps how they were able to come up with the points.

The game then continues with a search for hope. Most of the kids will realize that, according to the rules of the game (which cannot be changed), they have little hope. What they need is points—lots of them. After sufficient discouragement has set in, announce that you are going to give everyone 1,000 free points if they would like them and would take them. After all, it's your game and you can give points if you want to.

It doesn't take long for kids to see how God has done the same thing for us. That's what grace is (the free gift of God through his Son, Jesus). All we have to do is accept it through faith in him.

Larry Thomas

CROSSING THE RIVER

To what lengths do people go to avoid facing problems, or even death itself?

Outline with masking tape the two banks of an imaginary 20-foot-wide river that flows through your youth room. Sit your group on one side, designate a corner of that side as a cemetery, and seat yourself and a strong high school boy (on your right) on the opposite side. Now tell the kids across the river from you that their task is to figure out a way to cross the river without getting their feet wet. If they succeed, they sit with you; if they fail, they are consigned to the cemetery. Tell them that you have the final call as to their destiny. They have 10 to 15 minutes.

Your students will probably try lots of ingenious methods of getting over to you—erecting bridges of chairs and tables, piggy-backing each other, perhaps exiting through a door on their side in order to circle the church and enter a door on your side. All such attempts relegate students to the cemetery.

Finally, send your husky high schooler over to them, having clued him in to say, "The youth pastor says time is running out. If you want, I'll

How to Get to Heaven

HOW TO GET POINTS

1 point items:
- Good deeds done during the past week
- Books of the Bible memorized (in order)
- Each memorized commandment

5 points each:
- Each dollar given to the church or the poor during the past week
- Each time you prayed during the past week
- Each time you read the Bible during the past week
- Each church service attended during the past month

10 bonus points:
- Bringing a friend (nonmember) with you to church

50 bonus points:
- Knowing at least three Bible verses (with references)
- Memorizing one creed (for example, Apostle's Creed)

100 bonus points:
- Sharing Christ with someone during the past week
- Participating in a service project of some kind during past month (helping the poor, needy, etc.)

POINTS ARE DEDUCTED FOR THE FOLLOWING

1 point for:
- Each occasion of swearing during the week
- Each commandment broken this week (see Matt. 5)
- Disobeying parents this week

5 points for:
- Cheating on a test this past month
- Each day you didn't pray this week
- Missing Sunday school this month (per Sunday)

10 points for:
- Each lie told this week
- Every occasion of gossip
- Each day without reading the Bible

carry you over—but you must ask me." Then he returns to your side and waits, often while the group begins with "Carry him!" and "Carry her!" When one hits on "Carry me!" the assistant responds—but probably doesn't get many across before you say, "Time is up."

Circle together for a discussion, and introduce questions like these:

- What do people do to try to avoid dying?
- How do people try to get to God?
- What kind of more mundane problems do people attempt to solve—in vain—by their own wits or trust in another human?
- What feelings did you experience during the game?
- What analogies can you see in the game? (You—God the Father; strong high school boy—Jesus; river—death, separation from God; your assistant's message—the Gospel, which cannot be volunteered for any but oneself)

Brad S. Fulton

Door Jammin'

Door Jammin' is a physical reminder to students of the decisions they made for Christ.

Begin the event with a reading of Bible passages about doorposts (doorjambs) and doors (for example, Exodus 11:1-12:13, Deuteronomy 6:4-9), and spend some time explaining their importance. Discuss especially Acts 14:26-27—the "door of faith."

Then make a door of faith! Give the new converts permanent-ink pens and ask them to write their names and the dates of their commitments on the doorjambs of the youth room. Merely passing through the door will remind your group members of those new Christians in their group and what the Lord did for them. *Michael O'Neill*

SELF-IMAGE

Observation Game

Send a person out of the room. While he is gone, ask the others to tell things about the person's appearance. For example: What color is his shirt?

Does he wear glasses? What kind of shoes is he wearing? Write the facts down on a blackboard and have the person reenter. Compare with the descriptions.

Follow up with a discussion on how much we notice about each other. It might be a good idea to fix the person ahead of time—that is, give him some distinct things to wear, like a leather watch band, monogrammed shirt, etc. *Jim Olia*

Make a Melody

Reprint the musical note pattern on page 121 and distribute it to your group (one per person) with crayons or colored felt-tip markers. Have them personalize the notes with their names and any other writing or drawn design they like. The final product should reflect each person's uniqueness in some way.

Now collect the notes, and have the group choose together a hymn or other song that would serve as a good theme song for them. Later, find a simple arrangement of the theme they've chosen. Draw a large musical staff on a long sheet of butcher paper, hang it in a prominent place, and arrange the notes so that they form the melody of the group theme song. At your next get-together, talk about how just as every note is important to the song, every person is important to the group. *Brad Hirsch*

Identity Masks

Get some large grocery sacks and cut slots in each sack for eyes. On the sacks write (in red) different identities adolescents get in high school (one identity on each sack). Under these names, write down (in black) how they are to be treated (examples follow).

Give each person one of these masks, face down so they don't know what's on it. Have the students shut their eyes while they put the masks so they cannot see who they are. Tell them to mill around the room and interact with each other. They have two tasks: to treat each person according to the directions on the masks and to guess who they are from the interaction of others with them. Tell them to keep in touch with their feelings, especially their feelings about themselves. For best

MAKE A MELODY

Instructions: Color, design, or decorate your note any way you want. Be creative! You may want to use this note as a pattern for a construction paper note; collage a note; draw your face on it; etc. ... Make it YOUR note, personal and unique, just as your life is personal and unique.

Your life is a note and a song to Jesus: Sing and make melody in your heart to the Lord!

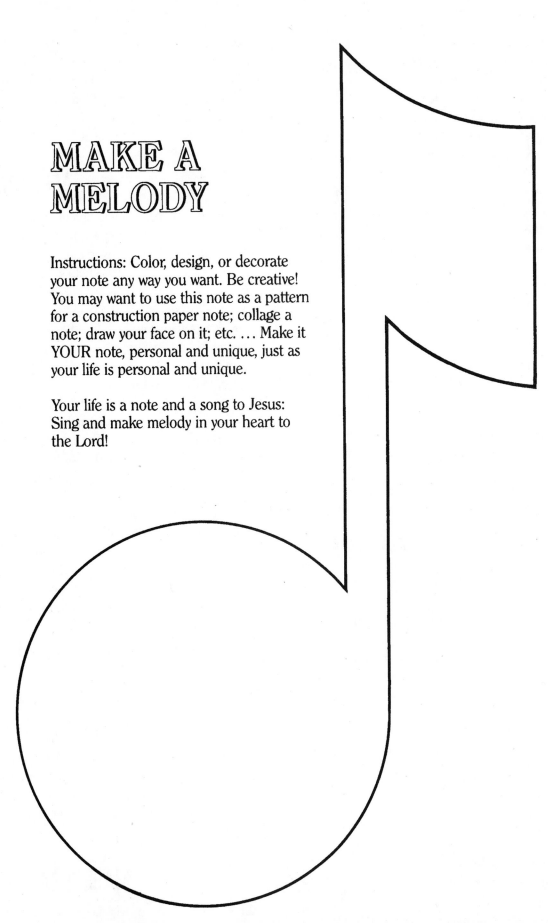

results give the negative labels to the most outgoing, accepted kids in the group and the positive labels to the quieter, less noticed ones.

Here are some ideas for masks:

• **Joe Cool**—ask me to parties, accept me, laugh at what I say, tell me how cool I am

• **Patty Party**—invite me to any social gathering, accept me, act wild and uninhibited around me

• **Betty Bod**—ask me out, accept me, flirt with me, tell me how good-looking I am

• **Jerry Jock**—tell me how strong I am, talk about sports around me, flirt with me, ask me to be on your sports team

• **Ivan Intellect**—respect me for my "smarts," ask me to sit by you in class, tell me how intelligent I am

• **Steven Stud**—ask me out, tell me how good-looking I am, flirt with me, accept me, get in good with me

• **Bryan Bookworm**—reject me, tell me I'm boring, poke fun at me

• **Ralph Runt**—kid me about being small, reject me subtly, act big around me

• **Andy Clutz**—reject me, tell about the dumb things I do, tell a joke about me

• **Paul Problem**—feel sorry for me, tell me how you understand, ask me if it's going better today, don't respect me

• **Susie Dumb Blonde**—treat me as spacy but flirt with me

• **Nelson Nerd**—reject me, make nasty remarks to me, make fun of me

• **Wanda Wallflower**—reject me, don't acknowledge me, don't speak to me even if I talk

• **Ms. Liberation**—accept me, tell me how good I am in sports, act free around me, but don't ask me out or tell me I'm pretty

• **Ted Tough Guy**—act afraid of me, ask me if I've heard any off-color jokes lately, try to get on my good side, ask me to help you get even with somebody

After the students have had a chance to mingle long enough for their new personalities to form, discuss how who we are comes from others' opinions of us. Also discuss how these labels are not our real selves. Show them God's view of us and how his opinion is the one that should shape our lives. *Gary Salyer*

APPEARANCES

The multiple-choice questionnaire on page 123 is an excellent discussion starter on the subject of personal appearance. Most kids worry a great deal about how they look, and this can help give some direction and substance to this natural preoccupation.

This questionnaire could be combined with some other appearance-oriented exercise or icebreaker for an entire meeting or program on this theme. Here are some suggestions:

• Start with a fashion show.

• Hang up photos of people who dress in a variety of styles and have kids try to make some conclusions about the values or lifestyles represented. The object is to determine whether or not there is a connection between outward appearance and the real person.

• Have the youth sponsors dress in a very sloppy or bizarre manner for the meeting—or just different from normal. Watch the kids' reactions.

• Encourage the kids to come to the meeting dressed in a different or unusual way. Kids can come in formal attire or as sloppy as possible or wearing their favorite clothes.

• Have a game or drawing in which the winner gets a gift certificate to a clothing store (you might be able to get this donated).

The questionnaire is the important part. Make sure everyone has a copy, and give the group 10 or 15 minutes to complete it. Then discuss the questions in small groups or with the entire group. Try to focus on principles that will help kids to care about their appearance without being obsessed with conformity, status-seeking, or being phony. *Dan Mutschler*

MASQUERADE MIXER

Give kids supplies to help them make masks—paper bags, marking pens or crayons, magazines, glue, scis-

MY APPEARANCE

Please answer these questions in order. Don't go back and change your answers; your initial response was probably most honest.

1. I think about my appearance...
   a. constantly.
   b. regularly.
   c. when it is called to my attention.
   d. rarely.
   e. never (even when looking in a mirror).

2. The money I spend on clothes and my appearance is...
   a. ridiculous.
   b. too much.
   c. about right.
   d. not enough.

3. I dress the way I do for church on Sundays primarily because...
   a. I feel most comfortable this way.
   b. it is what others expect.
   c. I don't want to be noticed or to stick out.
   d. I want others to notice me.
   e. I think God would be pleased.
   f. I was taught by my parents to dress this way.
   g. (fill in another reason)
   _____.

4. Quite honestly, I...
   a. judge people on the basis of their appearance.
   b. don't let appearance affect the way I think of people.
   c. let appearance affect the way I judge people some, and rightly so!
   d. try not to be affected by people's appearance but can't help it.

5. I dress the way I do at work or school because...
   a. I feel most comfortable that way.
   b. it is what others expect.
   c. I don't want to be noticed or to stick out.
   d. I want others to notice me.
   e. I think God would be pleased.
   f. I was taught by my parents to dress that way.
   g. I would lose my job or be kicked out of school if I dressed otherwise.
   h. (fill in another reason)
   _____

6. Please rate the seven reasons listed in Question 5 from best (1) to worst (7) reasons for dressing the way one does.

7. Most people in our society (culture)...
   a. are hung up on appearance.
   b. don't care enough about their appearance.
   c. have a good perspective on the importance of appearance.
   d. (fill in another viewpoint)
   _____.

8. If I could change one thing about my appearance, it would be _____
   _____

9. The reason I would change my appearance is that...
   a. I would impress others more favorably.
   b. I would be able to put my concerns about my appearance behind me.
   c. I would be better in sports.
   d. I would feel better physically.
   e. I would be more attractive to the opposite sex.
   f. (fill in another reason)
   _____

10. Please rate the following three items as to whether you think they
    (1) matter very much to God
    (2) matter very little to God
    (3) matter to God if they matter to us
    (4) Really don't matter at all to God.
    a. how I dress_____
    b. whether I am overweight or underweight_____
    c. whether I shower, shave, keep hair combed and cut regularly_____

11. A Christian in our society...
    a. should have about the same ideas as others in our society do about appearance. That is, there's little wrong with how our society thinks about appearance. True False
    b. should be distinctly different from most of society in the way he thinks about appearance. True False

12. When I am dressed distinctly different from others in a social situation, I feel...
    a. pleased.
    b. embarrassed and conspicuous.
    c. comfortable.
    d. (fill in another viewpoint)
    _____

sors, and the like. Depending upon your purpose, the masks can look humorous, realistic, or symbolic. You might have kids make masks to show how they think they will look 10 years from now, masks that show how they wish they looked, or masks that fit some other theme.

Then have kids wear their masks, sit in a circle, and explain what their masks represent. As kids finish explaining their masks, have them remove them. Gradually the entire group will become unmasked and kids will learn a great deal about each other in the process.

Use your own creativity as to how you choose to use this basic idea. It can be a simple mixer, or it can be used as a serious learning strategy that can be tied in with a discussion on phoniness, the wearing of masks, discovering who we really are, and so on. *Hal Herwick*

More than Just a Pretty Name

A number of books on the market list thousands of common names and their original meanings. Get one or more copies of a book like this (libraries usually have them), and try the following exercise with your group. Break into small groups and have the kids look up each other's names in the reference book and find out what each one means and the character quality that it represents. Then have them (as soberly as possible) use that meaning as a way of affirming and encouraging each other.

A second phase might be to have the kids choose a new name for themselves or for others in their group, based upon the meaning of a particular name found in the book. When you first present this, you can point out from many different places in Scripture how the meaning of a person's name was important and had great significance (Jacob's children, Hosea's children, Jesus, Peter, etc.) *John Collins*

Putting Myself in a Box

Here's a great way to allow kids to share some deep feelings about themselves with each other.

First, you'll need to get some boxes—not too big—so that everyone has one. You might try getting those shoebox-size boxes that department stores have by the thousands in their gift-wrapping department. It's not important that everyone has

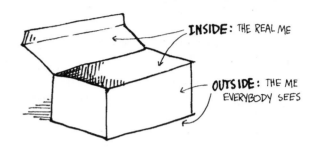

INSIDE: THE REAL ME

OUTSIDE: THE ME EVERYBODY SEES

the same size box, but it is important that the boxes are not too large. You'll also need some magazines, newspapers, scissors, glue, marking pens, and perhaps other craft materials.

After everyone has a box, explain that kids are to make a collage on the inside of the box that represents how they see themselves or how they feel about themselves. These feelings should be expressed through pictures, words, or symbols. On the outside of the box, they should make a collage that represents how they think others see them— how they are seen through the eyes of people who come in contact with them. If they want they can let each side of the box represent how different people or groups of people see them (they will often be different).

After the boxes have been made (be sure to allow plenty of time), let the kids get into small groups and share their boxes (essentially, they are sharing themselves) with each other. It will help kids to open up with each other in a relatively non-threatening way and provide a chance for kids to be supportive of one another.

Discussion can center on why there is a difference between the inside and the outside of the box and how we can improve both. *Eric Finsand*

Design-an-Image

If self-image doesn't concern your kids—or so they say—try this activity. Distribute copies of the illustrations on pages 125-126 and have teens follow the directions. An imaginative survey like this reveals to kids that most of them aren't completely satisfied with themselves. After redesigning themselves

You are the designer!

Write in each blank what you'd desire for yourself if you were the designer. If you're satisfied with a given aspect of yourself, simply write that down. When you've completed the chart, share with your group what things about yourself you'd change, what you wouldn't change, and why you chose what you did.

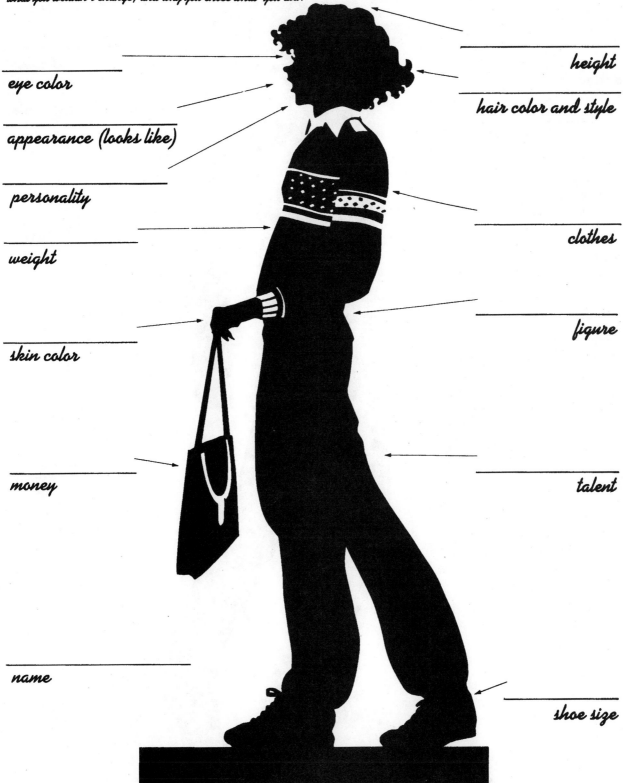

eye color

appearance (looks like)

personality

weight

skin color

money

name

height

hair color and style

clothes

figure

talent

shoe size

You are the designer!

Write in each blank what you'd desire for yourself if you were the designer. If you're satisfied with a given aspect of yourself, simply write that down. When you've completed the chart, share with your group what things about yourself you'd change, what you wouldn't change, and why you chose what you did.

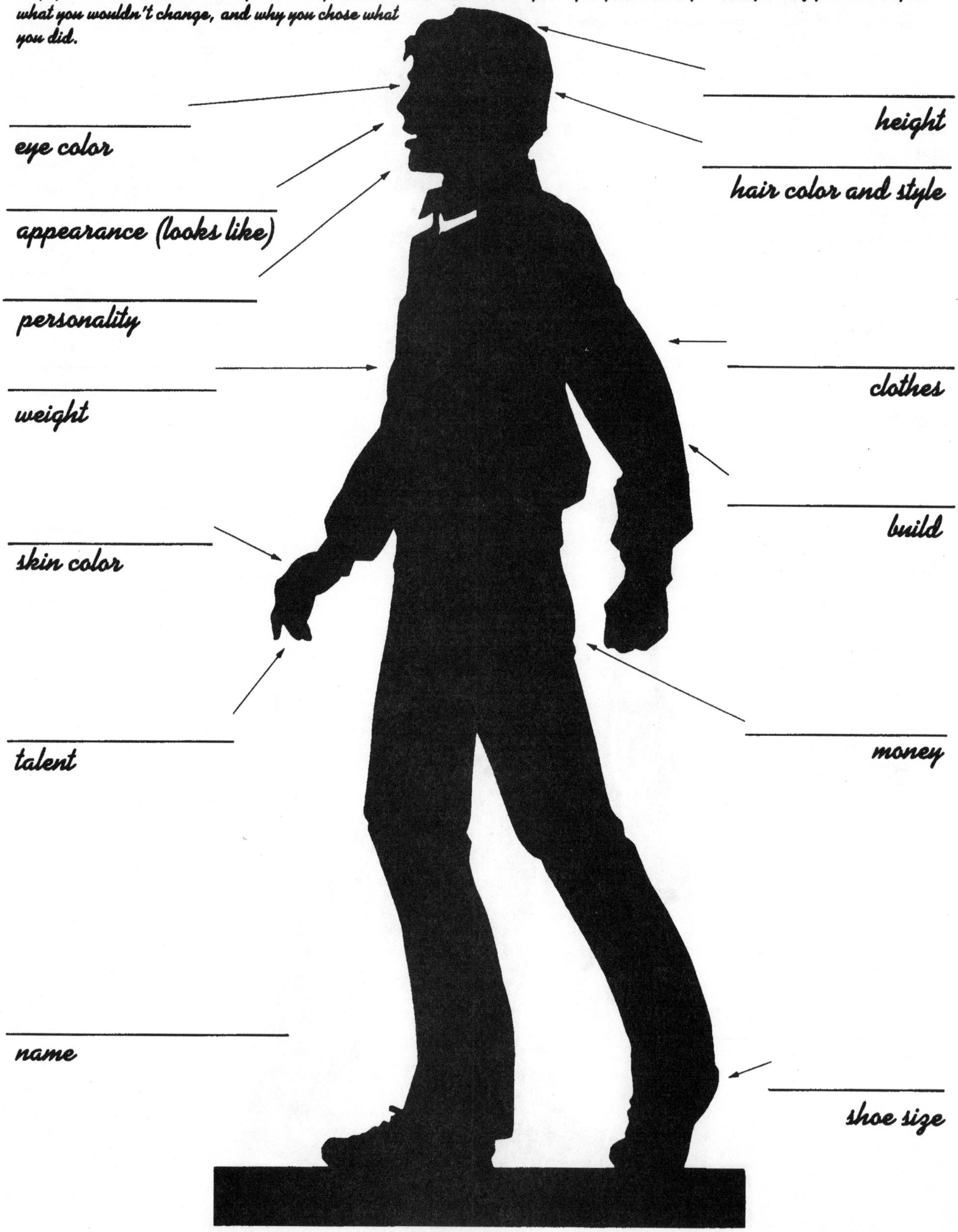

_____
eye color

_____
appearance (looks like)

_____
personality

_____
weight

_____
skin color

_____
talent

_____
name

_____
height

_____
hair color and style

_____
clothes

_____
build

_____
money

_____
shoe size

they're usually ready to learn about self-image and self-acceptance. *Kurt Staeuble*

Now That's Cool!

Here's an entertaining and thought-provoking way to help your kids rethink their expectations of themselves and others. Make an overhead transparency of the Average-Looking Guy on page 127. Then ask your kids to tell you how to make him look cool. As suggestions are made, you or one of the kids draw on the additions. The kids' changes may resemble these:

Updated hair style   Nike shoes
Earring   More muscles
Shades   Smaller nose
Six-pack of beer   Sports car

After the kids complete their cool person, you might discuss each feature and why it's so cool—or why it isn't.

It would be a good idea to make all your additions to the drawing on a second transparency that lays on top of the first. That way, the second one can be removed in order to demonstrate that we're basically the same on the inside, regardless  of how much cool stuff we layer on the outside.

This also helps to demonstrate that coolness is really a man-made myth, and that God doesn't care how cool we are. He looks at our hearts—what's on the inside—and so should we. *Joe Harvey*

Baseball Card Devotional

Have the kids in your group bring their baseball-card collections to the meeting and share information about their favorite cards, most valuable cards, unusual trades, and so on. You might invite a professional collector or dealer to the meeting to explain

why some cards are more valuable than others, how to collect cards as an investment, and so on.

With that introduction, the stage is set for a devotional using sports cards as an object lesson. Ask the group members to imagine that they are on a Christian card—a card with their picture on the front and biography and stats on the back. Here are some questions to pose for your group:

• The front of a sports card always captures the individual in a flattering, complimentary pose. If you were pictured on a Christian card, what would your card catch you doing—singing, marching, debating, cheerleading, sports, or—?
• What would the stats on the back of your card reveal about you? Most cards' stats begin with the year a player first entered the league; if the first year listed on your card was the year you accepted Christ or began your spiritual journey, what would the following years say about you, statistically?
• What makes some cards unusually valuable is the fact that they are "error cards"—that is, the publishers made a mistake on the card. Some detail on them is wrong. What mistake, failure, shortcoming, handicap, or lapse in your faith has given you opportunity to grow stronger and to become more valuable to the kingdom?
• When a player autographs his own card, its value increases. How have you put your signature on people and places around you? What kind of mark are you making on the world?

Wrap up with a discussion of 2 Timothy 4:7-8. *Kevin Wieser*

Now That's Cool!

WANNABE BINGO

Give one bingo sheet (page 130) and a pencil to each player, and let everyone mingle.

The object is for players to find people who want to be like the person or trait written in one of the squares, and then ask that person to put his or her initials in the appropriate square. The winner must get initials in four squares in one horizontal or vertical row or in one diagonal row. Players can initial only one square on their own bingo sheets. The rest of the squares must be initialed by different players. With a bigger group ask for two players to initial each square.

HIT PERSONALITIES

Their favorite songs can reflect teenagers' personalities and interests. So ask them to bring you the album containing their favorite song—but in a bag, to keep it secret from the others.

Either at that meeting or a later one, play at least part of each song, and let the group guess whose favorite it is. Then let that student (or students, since more than one may select the same song) explain how the song reflects his or her personality.

Write the song titles and the choosers' names on poster-board CDs to display on the walls.

Sherry Wingert

SERVING GOD

WAYS TO SERVE GOD

To help your youths think about how they can put their faith into action, distribute copies of the 10 statements on page 131. Have each person circle "T" for true or "F" for false beside each one. Then have a discussion based on their answers.

To explore the subject in more depth, break into small groups and assign each group one of these five topics to brainstorm:
• Ways to serve God in our personal lives
• Ways to serve God in our families
• Ways to serve God in our church

• Ways to serve God in our community
• Ways to serve God in the world.

Then let a spokesperson for each group report their ideas back to the entire group. By the end of the program, you'll have a long list of ways the youths can serve God. Type up the list and give it out at the next meeting. *Richard and Vickie Glazier*

SIN

WHATEVER HAPPENED TO SIN?

Here's a creative discussion and object lesson on sin and forgiveness. Begin with a discussion of sin, using questions such as these:

• **What is sin?**
• **Name several specific sins that come to your mind.**
• **What sins are considered acceptable with the group?**
• **Are some sins worse than others?**
• **How do you deal with sin? In what ways do you succeed and in what ways do you fail?**

After the discussion, ask the group: "Would you like to be sure of forgiveness for your sins? You can." Then pass out pieces of paper to everyone.

Ask the group to write down on the pieces of

paper any sins in their lives they still worry about. Tell the kids that what they write will only be seen

Wannabe Bingo

Instructions: Find people who match the traits or celebrities they want to be like. Ask them to initial that space. On your own sheet you can initial only one space yourself; others can initial only one space each. The object is to get four initialed squares in a row—horizontally, vertically, or diagonally.

A Great Actor	Stronger	Normal	Mr. Universe
Athletic	A Great Singer	Blonde	Taller
Blue-eyed	Thinner	More Motivated	Brown-eyed
Popular	Miss Universe	Prettier	Smarter

Ways to Serve God

T F   1. The only way to serve God is to be a pastor.

T F   2. You cannot serve God at school.

T F   3. If you're being paid for a job, it can't be service to God.

T F   4. Only certain people can serve God.

T F   5. We should serve God only on Sundays.

T F   6. Feeding ducks is serving God.

T F   7. Serving God may require sacrifice.

T F   8. Men serve God better than women.

T F   9. Driving the church van is serving God.

T F 10. Getting good grades has nothing to do with serving God.

by themselves and God, so they can be very specific and honest. After they have written down their sins, have them sign their names and write "Forgive me" under it. This will take some courage, so you need to reassure them all again that they will not be betrayed—no one will see the words except God.

Now ask them to fold up their pieces of paper and put them in an open coffee can which is up front. When all the sheets are collected in the can, talk about how Christ cleanses us from all our sins. You might want to read an appropriate Scripture at this point.

Then, to illustrate how Christ forgives and forgets, take a match, light it, and drop it in the can. There will be a flash and poof! The can is empty. Not even ash will be left. After everyone sees the can, explain that it is just like that with God's forgiveness, so they can "go and sin no more."

How is it done? The sheets of paper passed out are magician's flash paper, which can be bought at any novelty or magic supply store. When a flame is added, it literally vanishes. The can, by the way, should be placed on something that can take a little heat. *David Parke*

SOCIAL CONCERNS

PRIORITY GAME

Copy and hand out copies of page 133. Have the kids cut it into nine pieces. Explain:

These are causes for marching, causes for which people are giving at least part of their lives. You have two blank sheets for any other important causes you know of. Add these, then arrange the slips in order of importance to you. Do this carefully. You will have five minutes.

After everyone seems to have the paper slips in order say,

Get together with your neighbor and each of you tell the other what your first three were and why.

After three or four minutes ask some to share their first or second choice and why they

placed it first or second. They are not to criticize or evaluate another's order or reasons, only inform the other of their own order and reasons.

After hearing these, students may rearrange their own orders if they wish or they may leave them the same. Give them about two minutes for this. When they are finished say,

Your first three are the things that you each have said are the most important causes for which you could give your lives. Now on the back of the first three (and more if you have the time) write how you have spent your time during the last month in each.

When they are finished, ask how they felt when asked to write the above.

Then have them write down on the back of the first three (more if time permits) how they *plan* to spend time in the next month on each. Have them share their plans with one of their neighbors.

The purpose of this program is to make the kids think about what their priorities are and should be, consider their past actions, and plan and make a commitment concerning their future lives. Close with additional discussion and prayer. *Tom Barwick*

REAL WORLD GAME

The following simulation game can be used effectively prior to a discussion on poverty in the world, selfishness, war, international relations, or any number of relevant subjects. The game requires about an hour and a half and involves a somewhat realistic situation of survival centering around the grain production and needs of various countries. The game involves seven groups of six to 10 persons (adapt for your group size) with each group representing a country with designated grain production, grain needs per month, and monthly income.

You will need the following materials:
• 15 or more cups of grain (unpopped popcorn or whatever can be conveniently measured and handled)
• Three rolls of pennies (the income could be changed to dollars so play money could be used)
• Eight plastic measuring cups with graduations to ⅛ cup—the leader gets a cup and each country gets one cup
• Seven 3x5 weather cards with three of them hav-

The Priority Game

Peace in the World	Feeding the hungry	Civil Rights (Racial Discrimination)
Right-to-life movement (anti-abortion)	Concern for military buildups and spending	Ecology and concern for the environment
Equal rights for women	Evangelizing the world for Christ	Bringing justice for the poor and oppressed

---

Peace in the World	Feeding the hungry	Civil Rights (Racial Discrimination)
Right-to-life movement (anti-abortion)	Concern for military buildups and spending	Ecology and concern for the environment
Equal rights for women	Evangelizing the world for Christ	Bringing justice for the poor and oppressed

ing instructions (see the World Situation fact sheet on page 135)

• Eight copies of the World Situation fact sheet (on page 135), one for the leader and one for each country

Follow these procedures:
Most of the instructions are included on the World Situation fact sheet. However, the leader needs to keep a few additional things in mind:

• Have all the supplies distributed to each team before the preparation period begins in order to save confusion.

• Make sure taking the monthly consumptions and giving the monthly production and income is fully completed between each monthly time period before another time period is begun.

• Between each time period collect the weather cards and reshuffle them and have the presidents pick them randomly. This, too, should be done before a new time period is begun.

• It is important that the leader refrain as much as possible from giving additional instructions or answering questions once the game is in process. This will allow for more initiative by the players in tackling the task without depending on the leader to guide them toward a successful conclusion.

If your situation calls for a different number of countries than seven, then you will need to revise the World Situation Fact Sheet. In setting up a different situation, make sure the total production of all the countries is slightly more than the total needed. This will allow (at least theoretically) survival of every country. *W. Clarence Schitt*

THE GREAT DONUT CRISIS AND THE GREAT POPCORN CRISIS

Here are two similar simulation games that can help your group deal with the problem of world hunger.

Divide your students into three groups and distribute position papers (pages 136-141) describing the situation. Each group represents one of three mythical nations who are attending a food crisis summit conference. For the purposes of this game each nation's entire food supply is either donuts or popcorn.

Have each country read its position paper and then formulate a position statement. Then the

countries will meet together to hear statements from the other countries. After the three opening statements, the floor is open for general statements on how the crisis can be averted. Following an adequate period of discussion, a debriefing should follow discussing the real-world problem of hunger. *Ed Tarvin*

ROBIN HOOD

Here's a fun simulation game that can open up some good discussion on the subjects of giving, selfishness, anger, relationships, and more. Divide into three groups. One group is the Givers group; another is the Takers group, and the third is the Robin Hoods group.

Give everyone in the room five clip-on clothespins and have them fasten them onto their clothes anywhere they want as long as they're visible. When the signal is given to begin, each group moves about the room doing as its name implies. If you're a Giver, then you give the clothespins you have to others of your choice. If you're a Taker, then you take. If you're a Robin Hood, then you try to right the wrongs that are being done by stealing from the rich and giving to the poor.

After a few minutes of this, discuss what happened with the group. Ask questions like these:

• How did you like your particular role in the game?
• Did anything in the game seem unfair?
• Did you get angry?
• Did you ever want to change roles?
• How does this game compare with real life?
• Are there any real-life Robin Hoods around today?

E. Parke Brown

SPIRITUAL GIFTS

SPIRITUAL GIFT LIST

Make a list of all the gifts of the spirit found in Ephesians 4, 1 Corinthians 12, and Romans 12. Then have everyone in the group place the gifts in order from most important to least important and

REAL WORLD GAME

INSTRUCTIONS

THE GOAL: Your purpose is to survive as a nation in whatever way you choose: beg (foreign aid), borrow, buy, (or steal!)

PREPARATION: You will have 10 minutes to study the fact sheet and elect the following officers:
- *President*—to lead in deciding his country's policy and to negotiate with other countries that come to him. He may not leave his own country.
- *Ambassador*—to negotiate for his country in other countries. You may elect more than one ambassador if you feel the need.
- *Treasurer*—to keep track of and guard the grain and money.

METHOD OF PLAY: The game is played in 10-minute time periods representing one month. Each month you will receive your monthly income and grain quotas. At the end of each month, you will have your monthly consumption of grain taken away. Your job is to see that, in the 10 minutes allotted, you have accumulated enough grain to equal the consumption that will be taken away. There will be six periods of play.

When time is called at the end of each month, all play must stop; all inter-country communication must cease; all players must return to their respective countries.

At the beginning of each month, except the first, each country's president will draw a weather card; a clear card indicates good weather and no change in grain production; FLOOD AND DROUGHT cards mean your grain production is cut in half that month; BUMPER CROP means you have 1 cup extra (large grain producers) or ½ cup extra (small grain producers) that month.

STARVATION: If you haven't enough grain at the end of any monthly time period to meet your needs, your country starves and is out of the game.

World Situation Fact Sheet				
Country	*Direct Trading Countries	Monthly Grain Production	Monthly Grain Needs	Monthly Gross National Income
Canada	All Countries	2 Cups	½ Cup	3¢
China	Japan, Great Britain, Canada ONLY	2 ½ Cups	3 Cups	1¢
Great Britain	all but Russia	½ Cup	¾ Cup	3¢
India	all but China	¾ Cup	2 Cups	1¢
Japan	all but Russia	¼ Cup	1 Cup	4¢
Russia	India, Canada, United States ONLY	2 ½ Cups	1 ½ Cups	2¢
United States	all but China	2 ½ Cups	1 ¼ Cups	5¢

*Trading with countries that you're not allowed to trade with DIRECTLY, MAY be traded with through a neutral country acting as an intermediary. A neutral country is one that can trade directly with the countries that want to negotiate.

The Great Donut Crisis

INSTRUCTIONS

You represent one of three nations involved in a serious food shortage situation. All groups have 10 minutes to perform the following tasks:

- Elect a chairperson for your delegation.

- Inventory your nation's food supply and compare it to your needs.

- Examine the position statement below and decide what course of action your country should take.

- Your chairperson should be prepared to present a five-minute statement of position at the General Assembly and all members of the delegation should be ready to defend your nation's position.

POSITION STATEMENT

You represent the United States of Donuts.

You have plenty of food to feed your population and enough left over to export to other countries. Your problem is that your people do not want to give away your food to the needy. The donut makers want higher prices and everyone in your country is satisfied because they have all of the donuts that they can eat at prices they can afford.

What is your nation's position?

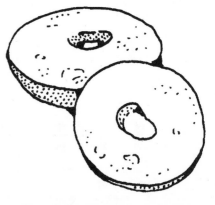

The Great Donut Crisis

INSTRUCTIONS

You represent one of three nations involved in a serious food shortage situation. All groups have 10 minutes to perform the following tasks:

- Elect a chairperson for your delegation.

- Inventory your nation's food supply and compare it to your needs.

- Examine the position statement below and decide what course of action your country should take.

- Your chairperson should be prepared to present a five-minute statement of position at the General Assembly and all members of the delegation should be ready to defend your nation's position.

POSITION STATEMENT

You represent the Republic of Bad News.

Your country has a population problem and most of your land area is not suited for agriculture. Furthermore, both your people and your government are very poor and cannot afford modern donut making equipment that is needed to feed your people. At the conference, you must look to the other two nations for help.

What does your nation have to offer in the bargaining? What is your nation's position?

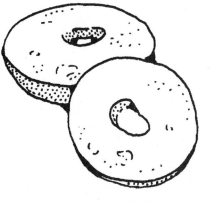

The Great Donut Crisis

INSTRUCTIONS

You represent one of three nations involved in a serious food shortage situation. All groups have 10 minutes to perform the following tasks:

- Elect a chairperson for your delegation.

- Inventory your nation's food supply and compare it to your needs.

- Examine the position statement below and decide what course of action your country should take.

- Your chairperson should be prepared to present a five-minute statement of position at the General Assembly and all members of the delegation should be ready to defend your nation's position.

POSITION STATEMENT

You represent the Federation of Big Business.

Your country cannot produce enough food but you have plenty of industry and money to import all that you need from the U.S. of Donuts. However, your economy depends on the sea route and ports of Bad News and you have been good allies with the Bad News Republic for over 100 years. You have called this confer- ence in your capital city to try to help in this crisis.

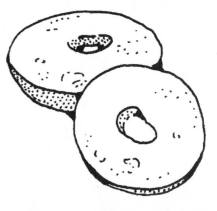

What is your nation's position and how will you persuade the United States of donuts to help your friends in Bad News?

The Great Popcorn Crisis

INSTRUCTIONS

You represent one of three nations involved in a serious food shortage situation. All groups have 10 minutes to perform the following tasks:

- Elect a chairperson for your delegation.

- Inventory your nation's food supply and compare it to your needs.

- Examine the position statement below and decide what course of action your country should take.

- Your chairperson should be prepared to present a five-minute statement of position at the General Assembly and all members of the delegation should be ready to defend your nation's position.

POSITION STATEMENT

You represent the People's Republic of Popcorn (P.R.P.)

You are a very rich agricultural nation which produces 90 percent of your continent's main foodstuff, popcorn. Of this popcorn crop, your country needs only 50 percent to feed itself, so that 50 percent is shipped out of the country. Most of those exports go to the United States of Hot Air, which supplies your country with most of its energy—hot air. The present crisis developed when the Kingdom of the Do-Withouts blockaded the Long and Winding River, thus cutting off the main trade route between your country and the U.S. of H.A.

Your assignment is to obtain the desperately needed trade route through the Kingdom of the Do-Withouts. Keep in mind that your nation is in need of more hot air and faces the chance of spoilage of this year's huge popcorn crop.

The Great Popcorn Crisis

INSTRUCTIONS

You represent one of three nations involved in a serious food shortage situation. All groups have 10 minutes to perform the following tasks:

- Elect a chairperson for your delegation.

- Inventory your nation's food supply and compare it to your needs.

- Examine the position statement below and decide what course of action your country should take.

- Your chairperson should be prepared to present a five-minute statement of position at the General Assembly and all members of the delegation should be ready to defend your nation's position.

POSITION STATEMENT

You represent the Kingdom of the Do-Withouts.

Your country is very poor and produces only five percent of the popcorn supply. This small amount will just barely supply the needs of 50 percent of your population. In the past, most of your government's money has gone to buy food to feed the starving people of your country. The popcorn is bought from the P.R.P. at very high prices.

However, there is now talk of spending that money on guns and patrol boats in order to completely control the Long and Winding River to force P.R.P. to lower its prices. The blockade has already begun. It is up to you to try to get more popcorn for your country. It should be noted, however, that every day of the military blockade is costing your country millions of dollars and causes more people to face the threat of starvation. You must decide how to act in the best interest of your people.

The Great Popcorn Crisis

INSTRUCTIONS

You represent one of three nations involved in a serious food shortage situation. All groups have 10 minutes to perform the following tasks:

- Elect a chairperson for your delegation.

- Inventory your nation's food supply and compare it to your needs.

- Examine the position statement below and decide what course of action your country should take.

- Your chairperson should be prepared to present a five-minute statement of position at the General Assembly and all members of the delegation should be ready to defend your nation's position.

POSITION STATEMENT

You represent the United States of Hot Air (U.S. of H.A.).

Your country is very small and mountainous and produces only five percent of the popcorn supply. This will feed only 50 percent of your population. However, your country has a supply of hot air, which is desperately needed by the People's Republic of Popcorn to run its popcorn factories. Now that the Kingdom of the Do-withouts has begun its blockade, you have a large supply of hot air but are running low on food to feed your hot air factory workers. Find a solution for your country's problem.

explain why they made their choices. Discuss the rankings in light of Paul's advice in 1 Corinthians 12:31 to "earnestly desire the greater gifts."

WHAT IS MY GIFT?

Here is a great way to focus on the discovery and use of spiritual gifts. Before the meeting print adhesive labels with descriptions of gifts—an usher, a good listener, a song leader, a Sunday school teacher, a caring friend, someone who bakes good cookies, someone who can repair books, a group leader, an intercessor, an organist, a pianist, an organizer, etc.

When the kids arrive place a gift label on their backs without telling them what it is. Tell everyone to mingle and ask others, "What is my

---

Good Listener

---

gift?" Others try to pantomime the answer and may say only "yes" or "no" in response to other questions. When someone discovers his gift, he can move the label to his arm.

Upon completion of this activity, discuss and evaluate each gift. Allow kids to exchange gifts for ones they feel better suited to. Or they can write their own ideas on a label. They can also place gift labels on others who they think have another gift. Some people may have one or two gifts—some more. The leader needs to make sure that everyone has at least one gift.

Then ask the following questions:

• What did it feel like to ask, "What is my gift?"
• What was it like to give someone else a gift?
• What was it like to receive a gift from another?

Pass an offering plate and have kids offer their gifts to God. Close with a prayer of dedication and thanks. *Doris Weber*

TRIPLE SPIRITUAL GIFT ASSESSMENT

This activity is a great way to encourage kids to recognize their gifts. The atmosphere is crucial: The group members need to feel relaxed, unhurried, and comfortable with one another.

Photocopy the list on page 143 so you can give one to every person. Keep in mind that this is not a list of skills or talents (cooks well or is a good athlete) but rather of character qualities.

Get kids to sit in a circle and ask them each to read the list and place a check beside the three gifts they feel best describe them. Then have them each place an "R" beside the three descriptions they think best apply to the person sitting to their immediate right. Finally, have them each place an "L" beside the three descriptions that best apply to the person on their immediate left.

Now have a volunteer read aloud the three descriptions he chose for the person on his right. Then let the student sitting on the other side of that person read the list for her also (that is, the two lists should be describing the same person).

Now have the person who has been described read the list for herself so the group can compare the results. Ask how that person felt about the choices made by the other two. Have the rest of the group add any other traits that might describe the person under discussion.

Repeat the process with the other kids in the group.

This may take some time, so if you have a large group, you may want to do a few people at each meeting for several meetings in a row. *Laura D. Russell, T. Carter Hiestand, and Gregory T. Foley*

GIFTEDNESS

Need to illustrate the value of the spiritual gifts God has given each of us? Choose eight volunteers; have them form two teams of four. Tell both teams that they have 10 minutes to build a house out of two sheets of paper. Give the first team their paper and send them to a separate room to work, emphasizing that they can only use the paper they were given—nothing else.

LIST OF TRAITS

_____ Compassionate

_____ Good listener

_____ Trustworthy

_____ Loyal

_____ Sympathetic

_____ Caring

_____ Cheerful

_____ Able to cheer up others

_____ Helpful

_____ Able to comfort people who are hurting

_____ Able to mediate between two people or groups

_____ Encouraging

_____ A good teacher

_____ Humorous

_____ Able to get things done

_____ Has plans for the future

_____ Hospitable—makes people feel comfortable

_____ Persevering/tenacious—able to hang in there

_____ Direct—doesn't play games

_____ Independent—is not easily influenced by fads or trends

_____ Nurturing—able to help people grow

_____ Organized

_____ Creative

_____ Tolerant—able to accept others without making judgments

_____ Diplomatic—able to see two sides of an issue

_____ Spiritual

_____ Humble

_____ Hopeful

_____ Optimistic

_____ Charitable—able to give everything freely

_____ Faithful

_____ Forgiving

_____ Sensitive

_____ Perceptive—able to see beyond the superficial level

_____ Other _____

_____ Other _____

_____ Other _____

After team one leaves, give the second team two sheets of paper—and also scissors, crayons, and tape. Now send that team to a separate room to work on their house.

Call the two groups to show off their houses. The team that received gifts will have produced a more interesting and intricate house than the team that received no gifts. Explain to the kids that in the same way God has gifted each one of us with spiritual gifts to build up our youth groups and churches to be the best they can be. *Kurt Staeuble*

SPIRITUAL WARFARE

OPENED EYES

All students receive four pipe cleaners each, make a pair of glasses from them, and wear the resulting pair of eyeglasses for the rest of the meeting.

Start a discussion this way: Suggest that all imagine what they might see if the glasses they are wearing enabled them to observe the spiritual realm clearly. What might they see when somebody dies? When conception happens? At a rock concert? What would heaven look like? Or the Devil? Or angels?

Follow up the discussion by studying spiritual warfare, emphasizing that God has given us authority over all the works of the enemy. Examine the Christian's armor in Ephesians 6:10-18, and tell the story of Elisha and his servant seeing the army of God surrounding them (2 Kings 6:15-17). Conclude the meeting by listening to part of the audio version of Frank Peretti's *This Present Darkness. Gene Stabe*

TELEVISION AND MOVIES

TV OR NOT TV

The questionnaire on page 145 is designed to stimulate discussion on the subject of television, the media, and its impact on our lives. The best way to use it is to divide the group into groups of three, and have each threesome fill out their questionnaire as a unit. Then have the whole group come back together for discussion and conclusions. *Dan Mutschler*

VIDIOTS UNITE!

A vidiot is a person who sits for hours at a time watching MTV with his or her brain in neutral. Unfortunately, many church kids are vidiots. Why not discuss the content and message of a few popular music videos with your youth group? Videotape a few selected ones and play them back for the group to watch together. Then discuss them, using the worksheet on page 146.

You can print up additional sheets for the kids to take home so they can fill them out for some of their favorite music videos. The purpose is to get the kids to begin thinking about what they are watching, in light of their faith. *David Carver*

TV AND THE TEN COMMANDMENTS

The next time you study the Ten Commandments, send a copy of the chart on page 147 home with your students. Have them note, with some details, what commandments they saw being obeyed and broken on TV.

When they return the following week with filled-in charts, discuss these and related questions:

1. What show televised the most number of obeyed commandments?
2. What show televised the most number of broken commandments?
3. Which commandments were broken most frequently?
4. What do you think the results say about the media?
5. What do your results imply about the viewers who support these shows?

Lyle Griner

TV or Not TV

1. How many hours a week do you watch TV? (average of each member of the group)_____

2. What one program is each member of the group most likely to watch each week? (list one for each member)_____
   _____
   _____
   _____

3. List three things you think have shaped your life and determined your values more than TV. List three that have had less influence. _____
   _____
   _____

4. List at least five ways TV has changed our society and affected our views of social issues, ourselves, others, and so on. _____
   _____
   _____

5. Rate each of the items you listed in Question 4 as "basically good," "basically bad," "neutral," or "questionable." _____
   _____

6. In what area of your life has TV most affected you?_____

7. If there were no TV, how would your life be different? What would you do without TV? ____
   _____

8. Can you think of any instruction given in the Bible that applies to your television viewing? Try to come up with several. _____
   _____
   _____

9. Could watching TV ever be considered a sin? When? _____
   _____

10. How can a person set guidelines for his own viewing? Write three rules that you think would be generally helpful for everyone. _____
    _____
    _____

Are You a Vidiot?

We all know what an idiot is. An idiot is a person who does things without thinking about them. When you call someone an idiot, it's an insult. A vidiot is almost the same thing. Vidiots let other people influence their minds without even asking questions about what they are watching. You are a vidiot if you continue to watch videos (MTV, etc.) for any period of time without stopping to think about what they are saying.

Today marks the first day of a campaign designed to make the vidiot an endangered species in our area. Please help us do this by watching some videos and then recording your thoughts about them on this paper. We can then discuss them together, eliminating the vidiot from this place.

As you watch the video and we discuss them, please keep in mind these verses from Philippians 4:8-9: "Here is a last piece of advice. If you believe in goodness and if you value the approval of God, fix your minds on whatever is true and honorable and just and pure and lovely and praiseworthy. Model your conduct on what you have learned from me, on what I have told you and shown you, and you will find that the God of peace will be with you." (Phillips translation)

NAME OF SONG _____

ARTIST _____

1. Did you like this video? Why or why not? _____
   _____

2. Did the visuals have anything to do with the song? _____
   _____

3. What was the song about? _____
   _____

4. What did the person singing the song want to happen? Is that a good thing to have happen? Why or why not? _____
   _____

5. As a Christian, do you think that this is a good video for someone to watch or listen to? Why or why not? _____
   _____

6. Does it fit the qualifications that Paul wrote about in Philippians? How? _____
   _____
   _____

TV AND THE TEN COMMANDMENTS

The Ten Commandments

1. You shall have no other gods before me.
2. You shall not make for yourself an idol.
3. You shall not misuse the name of the Lord your God.
4. Remember the Sabbath day by keeping it holy.
5. Honor your father and your mother.
6. You shall not murder.
7. You shall not commit adultery.
8. You shall not steal.
9. You shall not give false testimony against your neighbor.
10. You shall not covet anything that belongs to your neighbor.

	Name of character	Commandment obeyed	Commandment broken	Details
NAME OF PROGRAM ____ **DATE & TIME** ____				
NAME OF PROGRAM ____ **DATE & TIME** ____				
NAME OF PROGRAM ____ **DATE & TIME** ____				
NAME OF PROGRAM ____ **DATE & TIME** ____				
NAME OF PROGRAM ____ **DATE & TIME** ____				

MOVIE REVIEWS

As video rentals, cable television, and satellite TV increase in popularity and accessibility, young people will be watching more and more movies. Some satellite subscription services offer hundreds of viewing channels. In addition, more and more movies are being targeted directly at the adolescent audience.

In light of this trend, it's a good idea to teach kids how to watch a movie in a discerning manner. The worksheet below can be used by students to evaluate the movies they see in the light of Scripture.

To introduce the idea of learning to watch movies discerningly, rent a popular film and show it to your group. Let the kids know that in today's films, moviemakers don't use camera angles, lighting, background music, and so on haphazardly. Nothing is done without a purpose. So it can be very helpful to the viewer to understand the intent and purpose of a film.

After viewing the movie, have the kids fill out copies of the worksheet on page 149 and discuss their answers. Other questions that would be good for discussion might include:

1. Why is it dangerous to view a movie without thinking about what the film is really saying?
2. Will this movie help me in my relationships (to God, my family, my friends)?
3. What does this movie have to say about biblical norms for living?

David Carver

SEX IN THE MOVIES

Teenagers need to take seriously the effects sexually explicit material in movies can have on their lives. To generate discussion, ask some of the kids to tell their favorite movie or scene from a movie and why. Then tackle the questions on page 150 in small group discussion.

After the small groups come back together, have someone read aloud one or more of the following Scripture passages. Ask what light, if any, they shed on the subject under discussion.

Matthew 5:27-30
Ephesians 5:1-12
1 Thessolonians 4:1-8
Genesis 2:22-25; 3:1-12

In the large-group discussion that follows, point out or review some of the possible effects of viewing sexually explicit material. These might include the following: lust and inappropriate sexual arousal; guilt or shame; and questioning or rebelling against God's standards for sexual behavior. Encourage the kids to consider these and other possible effects when they're making decisions about film viewing. *David Wright*

VALUES AND MORALITY

THE WINDOW

Read or tell the story on page 151 to the group.

This beautiful story is not only an excellent illustration for a talk (on a variety of subjects) with its surprise twist at the end, but lends itself well to discussion. The following questions raise some possible issues.

1. What was your initial reaction to the story? Were you shocked? Surprised? Angry?
2. From the story, describe Mr. Wilson. What kind of man does he appear to be? Do you like or dislike him? Why?
3. Describe Mr. Thompson. What kind of person is he? Do you like or dislike him?
4. Why did Mr. Wilson do what he did? What do you think his motives were?
5. Would you describe Mr. Wilson's descriptions of what was outside the window as:
    (a) lying
    (b) creative imagination
    (c) unselfish concern for Mr. Thompson
    (d) cruel and envy producing
    (e) something else (please describe).
6. Did Mr. Wilson do anything wrong?
7. Why did Mr. Thompson's mood change from enjoyment and appreciation to resentment? Was his resentment justified?
8. Did Mr. Thompson murder Mr. Wilson?
9. Who was guilty of the more serious wrong? Mr. Wilson or Mr. Thompson?
10. Who was most responsible for Mr. Wilson's death? Why?
11. Would both men have been better off without Mr. Wilson's

How to Watch a Movie

Please view the movie with the rest of the group. While you are watching it, keep the following questions in mind—we will talk about them briefly afterward.

Remember, a movie is not made just for entertainment; there's a point to it. Let's see if we can discover it together.

1. Who is the hero of this movie? Why? _____
_____

2. Who is the villian or bad guy? Why? _____
_____

3. Is there an "evil" in this movie? That is, what is the bad thing that could or does happen (for example, the hero dies or the universe is destroyed)? How is that evil dealt with—what happens to it? _____
_____

4. Summarize the basic story of the movie in one or two sentences._____
_____

5. What do you think the producer and director are trying to communicate through this movie?
_____
_____

6. What does the Bible say about their message?_____
_____

7. Do you agree with what they're saying? _____

8. What happens during the movie that is in agreement with biblical teaching (for example, treating others kindly)? _____
_____

9. What happens during the movie that is in opposition with biblical teaching (for example, sex outside of marriage)? _____
_____

Thanks for answering these questions. I hope that you'll keep them in mind when you watch any movie, because you have to be careful about the stuff people are trying to teach you. I dare you to take a copy of this to the next movie you go see or to fill it out after the next movie you watch on TV. Try it. It'll be good for you, and once you get the hang of it, you'll enjoy movies a lot more!

SEX IN THE MOVIES

1. Do you think it's okay for actors and actresses to act in the nude or in sexually explicit scenes since they are only acting? Why or why not?

2. Why do you think movies today contain so much sexually explicit material? What is its purpose?

3. Do you believe that the movies present an accurate portrayal of sexual behavior or relationships between men and women?

4. Do you think Christians should attend or view sexually explicit films? Why or why not? Would the age or maturity of the viewer be a factor in this regard?

5. What kinds of effects might viewing sexually explicit scenes have on you? On your relationship to others? On your relationship to God?

SEX IN THE MOVIES

1. Do you think it's okay for actors and actresses to act in the nude or in sexually explicit scenes since they are only acting? Why or why not?

2. Why do you think movies today contain so much sexually explicit material? What is its purpose?

3. Do you believe that the movies present an accurate portrayal of sexual behavior or relationships between men and women?

4. Do you think Christians should attend or view sexually explicit films? Why or why not? Would the age or maturity of the viewer be a factor in this regard?

5. What kinds of effects might viewing sexually explicit scenes have on you? On your relationship to others? On your relationship to God?

THE WINDOW

There were once two men, Mr. Wilson and Mr. Thompson, both seriously ill in the same room of a great hospital—quite a small room, just large enough for the pair of them with two beds, two bedside lockers, a door opening into the hall, and one window looking out on the world.

Mr. Wilson, as part of his treatment, was allowed to sit up in bed for an hour in the afternoon (it had something to do with draining the fluid from his lungs). His bed was next to the window. But Mr. Thompson had to spend all of his time flat on his back. Both of them had to be kept quiet and still, which was the reason they were in the small room by themselves. They were grateful for the peace and privacy, though. None of the bustle and clatter and prying eyes of the general ward for them. Of course, one of the disadvantages was that they weren't allowed to do much: no reading, no radio, certainly no television. They just had to keep quiet and still, just the two of them.

Well, they used to talk for hours and hours. About their wives, their children, their homes, their jobs, their hobbies, their childhoods, what they did during the war, where they'd been on vacations, all that sort of thing. Every afternoon, when Mr. Wilson, the man by the window, was propped up, he would pass the time by describing what he could see outside. And Mr. Thompson began to live for those hours.

The window apparently overlooked a park with a lake where there were ducks and swans, children throwing them bread and sailing model boats, and young lovers walking hand in hand beneath the trees. And there were flowers and stretches of grass, games of softball, people taking their ease in the sunshine, and right at the back, behind the fringe of trees, there was a fine view of the city skyline. Mr. Thompson would listen to all of this, enjoying every minute. How a child nearly fell into the lake, how beautiful the girls were in their summer dresses, then an exciting ball game, or a boy playing with his puppy. He could almost see what was happening outside.

Then one fine afternoon when there was some sort of a parade, the thought struck him: Why should Wilson, next to the window, have all the pleasure of seeing what was going on? Why shouldn't he get the chance? He felt ashamed and tried not to think like that, but the more he tried, the worse he wanted a change. He would do anything! In a few days, he had turned sour. He should be by the window. He brooded. He couldn't sleep and grew even more seriously ill, which the doctors just couldn't understand.

One night as he stared at the ceiling, Mr. Wilson suddenly woke up, coughing and choking, the fluid congesting in this lungs, his hands groping for the call button that would bring the night nurse running. But Mr. Thompson watched without moving. The coughing racked the darkness. On and on. He choked and then stopped. The sound of breathing stopped. Mr. Thompson continued to stare at the ceiling.

In the morning, the day nurse came in with water for their baths and found Mr. Wilson dead. They took his body away quietly with no fuss.

As soon as it seemed decent, Mr. Thompson asked if he could be moved to the bed next to the window. So they moved him, tucked him in, made him quite comfortable, and left him alone to be quiet and still. The minute they'd gone, he propped himself up on one elbow, painfully and laboriously, and strained as he looked out the window.

It faced a blank wall.

descriptions of the view outside the window?

12. If you had been Mr. Thompson, how would you have felt when you finally looked out the window and saw nothing but a blank wall?

       (a) disappointed

       (b) angry

       (c) guilty

       (d) grieved

       (e) grateful

       (f) puzzled

       (g) shocked

13. Is it a sin to fantasize?

14. Is it a sin to hide the truth or to exaggerate when it doesn't hurt anyone?

15. Where does one draw the line in the areas of fantasy and imagination?

VALUES TEASERS

On page 153 you will find some stories and questions that can help your youth group think about what they believe. *Jim Walton*

CLEANING UP YOUR ACT

For a lively discussion on a variety of topics, have your group decide whether they agree or disagree with the 12 statements on page 154. When they have finished writing their personal responses, discuss each question individually and have the kids defend their positions. It would probably be wise for you as the leader to research and think through your own position on each one ahead of time. In addition, it would be a good idea to choose a few Scripture passages to help shed some light on the issues under discussion. *Steve Fortosis*

QUANDARY

This simulation ignites discussion about job ethics, family priorities, professional pressure, personal integrity, etc. Make copies of the story, responses and results (pages 155-156) for everyone in your group. Ask kids to work through this simulation silently. Tell them you will answer no questions. Then distribute the story and the responses to each student. When they have chosen their own responses, they should tell you the number of their response and get from you the corresponding result.

After everyone has arrived at a final response—whether it was forced or chosen—read the endings.

The Endings

Everyone choosing and remaining with response 1, or choosing response 1 followed by 6 with no others in between—this is your ending:

    After three weeks you are fired by your supervisor—but following a long letter to the executive officer in which you explain the problem, you are reinstated with a raise. Your supervisor is transferred to an out-of-state plant.

    The stories of all other final responses end this way: You hear nothing more about the matter until 18 months later, when you are questioned during an investigation of an industrial accident. A motor on a construction-site elevator burned out, stranding three workers on the steel 30 stories up as a storm with powerful winds approached. All three workers fell to their deaths.

    Here are some discussion starters following the simulation:

1. Were you responsible for the problem?

2. Was it fair that your job was jeopardized?

3. Do you think people are really put in situations like this?

4. What were your responsibilities in your job?

5. Rank in order of priority your obligations to the company administration, your supervisor, your workers, your family, consumers, stockholders, etc.

6. If you had it to do over, would you act differently? If so, why?

7. How will you decide what to do when you face choices like this in the adult world?

8. Look at Hebrews 12:2 and Revelation 3:21. If you decide to follow Christ's example, what will it cost you? What compensation is there?

Doug Thorne

LIFE AUCTION

Divide your students into small groups. Give each student a copy of the handout on page 157. After they have had a chance to determine their spending limits, bidding begins. After the auction, the whole group discusses and evaluates what happened.

PROBLEM HOTLINE

Have the group sit in a circle with two chairs back-to-back in the center of the circle. Choose two peo-

VALUE TEASERS

THE TALKING FRIEND. You and a good friend are both equally unprepared for a test, and together you cheat and pass. Your friend, however, begins to feel guilty about it and confesses to the teacher. In the process your friend implicates you as well and you both automatically fail the test.

- Should your friend have confessed?

- Couldn't your friend just have confessed to God and not the teacher?

- Should your friend have told the teacher about you?

THE BORROWING BROTHER. You and your brother share the same bedroom. You have made it very clear to your brother that he is to leave your belongings alone. You have a large CD collection and a stereo that you purchased with your own money. You come home from school one day and find many of your best CDs scattered on the floor and your favorite one has been stepped on. You blow up at your brother, and he apologizes and offers to buy a new CD, but you're still furious. You threaten to tell your parents about it and refuse to accept his apology. You tell him to get out of your room. Finally he has enough and says to you, "I know that you have been seeing Linda even though Mom and Dad told you not to. You have been telling them that you get off work at 10:00 but you really get off at 9:00. And if you keep yelling at me and threatening me, I'm going to tell them what I know."

- What's wrong with not wanting to let others use valuable possessions that might be wrecked?

- Which person in this situation is the worst in your opinion? Why?

- Is blackmail wrong?

THE CHANGING PARENTS. One evening a couple of your friends come by and you decide to attend a movie the next weekend. You ask your parents, and although they have never heard of the movie, they give their permission. The next Friday night your friends come to the house to pick you up, and your folks ask where you are going. You remind them that they had given you permission to go to a movie. Your dad responds, "Well, I did some checking, and I was going to talk to you. I forgot you were going tonight. But from what my friends tell me, the movie is no good. It contains a lot of profanity and explicit sex, so I don't think you can see it. Sorry, but you can't go." Your friends look at each other with shock and amazement. They can't believe it. Just as they leave you see them smile at each other like they think your folks are real losers. You are embarrassed, humiliated, and angry.

- Did your parents do the right thing?

- Do parents have the right to change their mind at the last minute?

- If you were a parent, how would you have handled the situation?

- If your parents would have done something like that, how would you have responded?

Cleaning Up Your Act

Read the following statements and mark your position on the agree/disagree continuum.

1. Pigging out is as wrong as smoking or drinking.

2. While you were walking home one night, a thief jumped from the shadows and demanded all your money. You gave your wallet to the man. He looked in the wallet and asked, "Is this all the money you have on you?" You said, "Yes," and the thief left with bitter threats. You had lied to the man; you had a 20 tucked away in your shirt pocket. Was that wrong?

3. To goof off on your job is as wrong as stealing money from your boss.

4. There are degrees of sin with God, so he doesn't really sweat the little sins we commit.

5. As Christians we are to obey all people who are in a position of authority over us, including policemen, parents, and teachers.

6. You're late for church, so instead of driving within the 40-mile-per-hour speed limit, your dad drives 55. Because you are rushing to a worship service, this is not wrong.

7. Going into your history final, you're just squeezing by with a C. Passing or failing this test could mean the difference between passing or failing the course. During the test you get a few answers from a friend's paper. As you walk out after the test, you know you have failed the test. In this case it is not necessary to confess cheating to the teacher.

8. God made man and woman for each other. God has also created some very attractive bodies. It's okay to lust after someone you see because actually you're just admiring God's creation.

9. A girl is very much in love with her boyfriend and he has said he loves her so much he would like to marry her eventually. Because she's in love and expects to marry this boy, her body belongs to him for the asking.

10. There is a guy at school who really gets on your nerves. Every time you see him you could punch his lights out. In fact, sometimes you wish he didn't exist. The bitterness you have for this guy is as sinful as if you actually killed him.

11. God doesn't exactly expect you to live as much like Jesus at home as outside the home. After all, we are supposed to be witnesses to all the world, not to our own family.

12. Jesus whipped the money-changers in the temple and chased them out. So it's okay to be obnoxious or cruel if the other person deserves it.

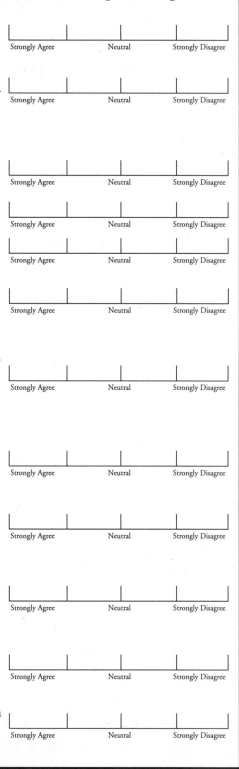

Story

You work for a company listed on the New York Stock Exchange that manufactures electric motors. You have a desk job in an office from which you oversee production on the night shift. You've been over-budget for a few months, thanks to having to pay some employees overtime to cover for others who've been sick. Your supervisor has consequently ordered you to bring the next month in under budget.

One of your crew chiefs comes to you secretly one night to inform you that the windings on the last gross of motors that his crew has put the covers on were made from a quality of wire slightly below specifications.

What do you do?

Possible Responses
(choose one)

1. Thank your crew chief, then circulate a memo to stop shipment until motors with the proper wire can be built.
2. Thank your crew chief, then call your supervisor for advice or intervention.
3. Tell your crew chief to mind his own business.
4. Tell your crew chief to call your supervisor and make the same report to him.
5. Thank your crew chief but do nothing, since the motors are so close to specifications that no one will ever know the difference.
6. Find another job, then resign.

Results

1. Word gets around the plant that the company has fallen even further behind. Your supervisor, now more frustrated, calls up to remind you of his order: more production, less expenses. When you tell him about the slightly lower quality of the last batch of motors, he gets irritated and snaps, "Your job is to make motors! If you can't do it, we'll get someone who can!" and then hangs up.

   How serious was he? Will you ship those motors if it means getting closer to your normal production quota? What will you do now? You may select another choice, or stay with this one.

2. Your supervisor is out of the office for the week. You must make another choice.

3. Your crew chief responds, "Whatever you say. I just wanted you to know." He walks out—and you begin wondering if he will report this to your supervisor or to one of the inspectors. You may select another choice or stay with this one.

4. Your crew chief says, "I'm afraid I'll lose my job if anyone besides you finds out that I told." He walks out. You must make another choice.

5. You hear nothing more about the matter. This is your final choice.

6. After about three weeks you find another company that hires you. This is your final choice.

LIFE AUCTION

You have received $5,000 and can spend the money any way you desire. Budget the money in the column labeled Amount Budgeted. We will then bid on each item in an Auction manner. Your goal is to gain the things you most desire.

	Amount Budgeted	Amount Spent	Highest Bid
A wonderful family life without any hassles.			
All the money I need to be happy.			
Never to be sick.			
To find the right mate, who is good-looking and fulfills me.			
Never to have pimples.			
To be able to do whatever you want whenever you want.			
To have all the power the President has.			
To be the best-looking person.			
To have a real hunger for reading the Bible.			
To be able to understand all things.			
To eliminate all hunger and disease in the world.			
To walk close to God always.			
Never to feel lonely or put down.			
Always to be happy and peaceful.			
Never to feel hurt.			
To own a beautiful home, car, boat, plane, and seven motorcycles (one for each day of the week).			
To have a genius IQ and never have to attend school.			
To be able to excel quickly and be superior in all things.			
To be filled with God's presence in the most dynamic way.			
To know that you are always in God's will.			
To be the greatest athlete in the world.			
To be looked up to by everyone else.			
To become a star on the most popular television show.			
To have a lot of close friends who never let you down.			

ple: one to be the Hotline worker, the other a caller with a problem. The worker leaves the room while the group leader assigns a problem to the caller. When the worker returns the caller pretends to call the worker and explain his problem. It is important that the worker and caller remain back-to-back. The group leader is responsible for cutting the mock call off at the proper time and leading a discussion among the rest of the group about how the problem might be solved.

Some examples of problems:

• I am not very attractive. People avoid me and I can tell that most of the people I know make fun of me behind my back. Frankly, I'm ugly. I know it and so does everyone else. So what can I do?

• My parents make me go to church. I like the youth program, but the worship service is a drag. Our minister is irrelevant and boring and the services don't relate to me at all.

• My mother is dying of cancer. Every day I am faced with cancer's ugly and depressing toll on my mom. I am forced to accept more and more of her responsibilities at home. But I like to go out with my friends, too. I feel guilty when I go somewhere and have a good time, but if I stay home I get angry and frustrated. What's the answer?

• I have always been told that kids who do drugs and drink really don't enjoy it. So I have refrained from doing those things partly because I believed that and partly because I didn't think it was a Christian thing to do. At least until a few weeks ago. I tried drugs and drinking and it was great. I never had so much fun in my life. How can something so good be bad? Were the people lying who told me how bad these things were?

Tom Grove

THE SECRET

• **The Background.** Mr. and Mrs. Benjamin are close friends with Bob and Lisa Sanders. Both couples are long-time members of the same church, pastored by Reverend Evans, who is married to Christine.

All three couples are having dinner at the Benjamin's house Saturday night. A few days before the dinner, while Mrs. Benjamin is out shopping, she notices a commotion at the exit. Apparently, someone was stopped for shoplifting. To Mrs. Benjamin's amazement that someone is Lisa

Sanders. Shocked and embarrassed, Mrs. Benjamin darted out of the store not knowing whether Lisa saw her or not.

Mrs. Benjamin feels very close to Lisa and plans to discuss the matter privately with her. But she is worried that such a discussion might damage their relationship.

Mr. Benjamin does not think his wife should mention it and believes it should be forgotten.

Bob Sanders has no idea his wife is shoplifting and the knowledge of such would be humiliating to him and he would have a difficult time understanding or forgiving.

Lisa Sanders knows that Mrs. Benjamin saw her and wants desperately to get help from her friends but is afraid her husband, Bob, could not handle it.

Reverend Evans is totally unaware of Lisa Sanders' problem.

Christine Evans has a difficult time accepting that Christians sin—especially a sin like shoplifting.

• **The Situation.** Just as the three couples sit down for dessert, a teenage son of the Benjamins runs in saying loudly, "Hey, mom, Sonny just told me that Mrs. Sanders got arrested for shoplift—" (he suddenly sees Mr. and Mrs. Sanders).

• **The Role-Play.** Chose students to act out this situation. When you feel enough has been said, stop the role-play and discuss what happened. Ask the actors to discuss what they were feeling and then get comments from the group. *Bruce Otto*

SOLOMON'S COLLAGE

Conduct a study of Ecclesiastes 2, which describes Solomon's vain experimentation with pleasure (sex, entertainment, alcohol), possessions (homes, land, wealth), and even the accumulation of wisdom and knowledge. This can be compared with how modern advertising still tries to convince the public that self-gratification leads to happiness. Distribute magazines, scissors, marking pens, and glue to the group and have them compose collages using advertisements and quotations from the Scripture text to communicate what they learned. This can result in a very impressive and thought-provoking display for the church lobby or youth meeting room. *Ron Rosenau*

TORTOISE AND THE HARE

This is a fun little discussion starter that could serve as an icebreaker in a larger discussion on the importance of each person in the body of Christ.

Give your group two categories such as Turtles and Rabbits. Ask them to decide which of the two categories they would rather be. Those that decide to be Turtles go to one side of the room and Rabbits go to the other side of the room. Then have each group discuss why they chose their category and make a list of their reasons. Then have a volunteer from each group read back their list of reasons. Combine everyone into one group again and give two new categories, repeating the entire process. Here are some suggestions for categories:

Volkswagon	Cadillac
River	Lake
Multimillionaire	President
Black	Oriental
Tall	Short

You can come up with many other categories. After you have done this exercise a number of times, bring the group together and discuss the problems of accepting people's circumstances and learning to accept our own circumstances. *Scott Wilson*

GILLIGAN'S ISLAND

This is an interesting values exercise that will allow your group to look at their own values and the values of others. Divide your group into small groups (six to eight people), read them the situation, and give them copies of the handout on page 160. They have 20 minutes to decide what items to throw overboard.

The Situation
You are all passengers on the luxury cruiser Majestic Prince, and after six days out at sea in the South Pacific, the ship suddenly strikes a coral ridge and begins to sink. Lifeboats are lowered and people begin to sail away from the sinking vessel.

Off in the distance is an island that your lifeboat hopes to land on, but your lifeboat is overcrowded and overweight, and you must throw off some of the supplies if you are going to make it to the island. If you don't, the boat will sink before you reach the island and everyone will be attacked by sharks or eventually drown.

In order to keep the lifeboat afloat, you must throw off six items from the list of heavy items and four from the list of light items. What you decide to keep will determine how you will live on the island, and could be the difference between life and death. So, make your choices carefully!

Steve Christopher

RIGHT AND WRONG

Display a poster like the one illustrated below before the entire group. Remove it after everyone has read it to themselves. They should not discuss it yet. Then pass out pencils and paper and have them write out the phrase they just saw. Chances are very good that most of the kids will be wrong. Most people don't notice that the word A is included twice.

Follow up with a discussion on how easy it is to be mistaken about something, even when you are sure you are right. Focus particularly on how we see only what we want to see; how we tend to go along with the majority—even when it is possible that they may be wrong; how we often make decisions based on preconceived ideas or on wrong information; etc. Discuss strategies for making right decisions and for determining right from wrong. *John Marchak*

COLORADO OR NEW YORK?

This is an exercise that gets people thinking about who they are and what they value. It is also a good community-builder as it helps open up group members to each other in a nonthreatening way.

Pass out the "I Am More Like…" handout

Gilligan's Island Time to Choose

Choose six items from the heavy list and four items from the light list to throw overboard.

Heavy items:

Case of unmarked sea rations

Fire extinguisher

Shovel

Blankets

Coil of rope

Five gallon can of fresh water

Cooking utensils (pots, pans, etc.)

Axe and sheath knife

Box of flares

Gas cooking stove

Light items:

Flashlight

Container of soap

First aid kit

Box of matches

Compass

Reflector mirror

Scissors

Canteen of fresh water

Transistor radio

Toilet paper

- -

Gilligan's Island Time to Choose

Choose six items from the heavy list and four items from the light list to throw overboard.

Heavy items:

Case of unmarked sea rations

Fire extinguisher

Shovel

Blankets

Coil of rope

Five gallon can of fresh water

Cooking utensils (pots, pans, etc.)

Axe and sheath knife

Box of flares

Gas cooking stove

Light items:

Flashlight

Container of soap

First aid kit

Box of matches

Compass

Reflector mirror

Scissors

Canteen of fresh water

Transistor radio

Toilet paper

(page 162) and ask them to circle the word in each pair that they feel they are most like (not what they would rather be). Tell them to circle the one they would most often feel like or choose. Ask them to think of the analogy between each of the two items or of what connotations come to mind as they try to decide between the two.

Explain that one item is not necessarily better than the other, only different.

For example, on item 1, the choice is between Colorado and New York. These two places bring to mind two distinctive environments or personalities. The idea is not to choose your favorite place or which one you would rather visit, but which one you are most like. Maybe you are most like New York because you have a lot of things going on in your life or because you are an exciting person. Or you may be more like Colorado, because you see yourself as quiet and alone or majestic and solid (like the Rocky Mountains) or as clean, uncluttered, or refreshing. Got the idea?

After everyone has completed the exercise, go over each number and have the students raise their hands if they feel they are more like the first item than the second. Then have those who feel they are more like the second item also raise their hands. Have them discuss the analogies they saw between the two items, and give them the opportunity to share why they picked the item they did. Some questions for further discussion:

• Do you ever feel threatened when you discover that your values are different from someone elses? Why? Do you think that God wants us to all have the same values, tastes, and personalities?
• Do you think that some of the choices on the list are more Christian than others?
• How did your interpretation of the items on the list make a difference in which one you chose? What does this say to us about the value of communication and trying to understand each other better? Can a person's interpretation and first impressions have anything to do with the way we accept and relate to others?
• After this exercise, are there certain items that you would like to change? Are you unsatisfied with the way you see yourself right now? What can a person do to change?
• How does our own self-awareness (how we see ourselves) affect the way we relate to others? How we relate to God?

Anna Hobbs

THE THIR-TEEN COMMANDMENTS

You can tie in this activity with a study of the Ten Commandments. Have small groups of kids create their own specific commandments that would apply to teen life today, such as "Thou shalt not cheat on exams" or "Thou shalt choose friends carefully."

As a large group decide which ones qualify as the winners and make them your official commandments named the Thir-Teen Commandments or the Four-Teen Commandments or another clever title. Rank them in order from the easiest commandment to obey to the hardest and discuss how to apply them in practical ways everyday. *Kevin Richardson*

SITUATION RESPONSE

Here is a game to get your kids thinking about how they respond to compromising situations. First, copy the response cards on page 163.

Have the group sit in a circle, then tell them you're going to present some imaginary situations in which they might one day find themselves. Tell them that you want them to respond to the situations according to the instructions they'll be given on the response cards. Then read the cards aloud, mix them up, and distribute them.

After each situation is described, have the card holders role-play a response according to their instructions. Let the rest of the group guess which card each person was given. Then collect the cards, mix them up again, and distribute to a new set of role-players.

Here are some sample situations to describe:

1. A good friend asks you for an answer during a biology test.
2. You're standing around with the gang, everyone else is smoking, and someone offers you a cigarette.
3. You're invited to a keg party at the beach.
4. At the checkout counter in the neighborhood convenience store, a busy cashier hands you change for a $20 bill, but you had only given her a $10 bill.
5. You watched TV instead of doing your homework last night. This morning a friend offers to let you copy her paper.
6. A friend tells you that he found out someone's locker combination and suggests that the two of you break into it when no one's around.
7. A conversation turns into gossip about one of your friends.

I Am More Like...

1. Colorado...New York
2. Volkswagen...Mercedes Benz
3. Leaky faucet...Overflowing dam
4. Moonlight...Firelight
5. Politician...Philosopher
6. Mountains...Desert
7. Marathon runner...Sprinter
8. Silk...Flannel
9. Dove...Eagle
10. Tug boat...Sailboat
11. Easy chair...Wooden bench
12. Oil painting...Snapshot
13. River...Lake
14. Paved highway...Rocky road
15. Hand...Eye
16. Lock...Key
17. Filing cabinet...Bulletin board
18. Tire...Steering wheel
19. Arrow...Bow
20. Music...Dancer
21. Collector...Dispenser
22. Golfer...Sky diver
23. Checkbook...Treasure chest
24. Social worker...Business executive
25. House...Tent
26. Fall...Spring
27. Jaguar...Snail
28. Violin...Trumpet
29. Morning...Evening
30. Wax...Rock
31. Cream cheese...Hot sauce
32. Comedian...Lawyer
33. Coal...Diamond
34. Lamb...Fox
35. News report...Soap opera

SITUATION RESPONSE

1. Respond by doing immediately what you know is wrong, then try to justify your behavior.

2. Respond with hesitation, debating with yourself about what you should do, then give in to what you know is wrong.

3. Respond by refusing to do wrong but acting judgmentally toward others involved.

4. Respond by refusing to do wrong, but refuse for the wrong reasons.

5. Respond by lying to avoid conflict or the consequences of your behavior.

6. Respond by refusing to do wrong and tactfully correcting others involved.

7. Respond by immediately doing wrong and then feeling sorry for what you did.

SITUATION RESPONSE

1. Respond by doing immediately what you know is wrong, then try to justify your behavior.

2. Respond with hesitation, debating with yourself about what you should do, then give in to what you know is wrong.

3. Respond by refusing to do wrong but acting judgmentally toward others involved.

4. Respond by refusing to do wrong, but refuse for the wrong reasons.

5. Respond by lying to avoid conflict or the consequences of your behavior.

6. Respond by refusing to do wrong and tactfully correcting others involved.

7. Respond by immediately doing wrong and then feeling sorry for what you did.

Add your own situations, or have the kids make suggestions themselves. They may even want to describe real situations they've experienced first-hand (no names should be mentioned). After you've spent as much time in role-play as you wish, discuss with the kids which response was easiest, most difficult, most natural, or most likely, and why.

Joe Harvey

CULTURE BOX

Here's a variation of show-and-tell that appeals to teenagers. During the week have all the kids make a culture box filled with items that typify their school culture to them, things that are important to them in their world—a football, a beer can, a CD of their favorite musical group, a friend's picture or anything that represents the world they live in.

When they bring their culture boxes with them to the meeting, have them divide into small groups and share their items one at a time, briefly explaining why they chose them. Ask the kids to comment on each one—how their things affect them, whether they're good or bad, etc.

This simple exercise is a great way for kids to examine their world and to discuss the contrasting values of their culture and of Christ. *Scott Oas*

SPIRITUAL VISION TEST

Use the test on page 165-166 to move your group to evaluate their spiritual condition. After they've taken the test, read aloud the diagnoses and discuss the Scriptures that apply based on their test results.

Larry Stoess

THE ISLAND AFFAIR

This activity can effectively help young people discover their beliefs and convictions as they react to

this story and answer questions about the characters in it.

Draw a large version of this diagram on the board; then tell the story on page 167.

After hearing the story, have kids get into small groups and rank the characters from "best person" to "worst person." A spokesperson from each group explains the group's choices. Good discussion can follow.

Further discussion can revolve around the following questions.

- Was Carla justified in what she did to be with Albert? Should she have accepted Bruno's proposal?
- Should Albert have accepted Carla? If Albert were a Christian, would he have behaved differently?
- Was Della's advice acceptable? If not, what advice would you have given?
- Is there any justification for Edgar's action?
- Why do you think Bruno accepted Carla? Would you have accepted Carla?

STANDING UP FOR YOUR VALUES

Make six colored squares out of cardboard, large enough for several of your kids to stand on. The colors of the six squares, and their positions, should look like this:

Red	Orange	Yellow	Yellow-Green	Green	Blue

Next, think up a number of hypothetical situations that involve making value choices, such as, "A baby is born with a serious birth defect that would make the child unable to live without constant care in an institution. Should the child be allowed to die?" Or, another example, "A woman is a prisoner in a concentration camp. Her husband and children are waiting for her in a nearby neutral country. The only possible way she can be freed from this prison is to become pregnant (the authorities automatically release pregnant women). Would it be right for her to have sexual relations with another man so that she can become pregnant?"

The young people are to decide what they think, and then stand on one of the colored

SPIRITUAL VISION TEST

Measure your spiritual vision with this spiritual test.

1. When you look in the mirror, what do you see? (Ps. 139:13-16)
   a. The handiwork of God
   b. Zits

2. When you are walking in the woods and come across a mulberry bush, what do you see? (Ex. 3:1-3)
   a. The burning bush of Mt. Horeb
   b. Mulberries

3. When you lay on your back in an open field and look into a cloud-filled sky, what do you see? (Ps. 19:1)
   a. The majesty of God
   b. A chance of rain

4. Which of these most resembles God to you?
   a. A rainbow
   b. A thundercloud

5. What do you see in this picture?
   a. A devil
   b. A kitten

6. In this picture the glass is—
   a. Half full
   b. Half empty

7. What do you see in this picture?
   a. Three crosses
   b. An algebra equation

   $$12 \,\dagger\, yx \,\dagger\, AB^2 \,\dagger\, 3 =$$

8. What do you see in this picture?
   a. A cross on its side
   b. An asymetrical X

9. When you see a driver cut you off, then direct an obscene gesture at you, what's your reaction?
   a. A feeling of compassion for someone so driven by anger.
   b. To return an obscene gesture.

10. What do you see in the numerals below?
    a. The combination to a gym locker
    b. A girl's statistics

    34   26   34

11. What is your reaction when you're in a group that's passing along bad but true gossip about someone you know?
    a. Suggest that there are two sides to every story, and that you're withholding judgment until you talk to the acquaintance personally.
    b. Just listen—and be thankful you're not the subject of this gossip.

12. What do you see in this picture?
    a. Money to help someone in need
    b. Money to spend on yourself

13. When you look at peoples' faults, what do you see first? (Matt. 7:1-5)
    a. The log in your eye
    b. The speck in their eye

14. What kind of movies do you like to see?
    a. Movies about adventure or relationships
    b. Movies characterized by sex or violence

15. Which would you rather watch?
    a. Sunsets
    b. TV

16. Which would you rather watch?
    a. PBS nature documentaries
    b. "Days of Our Lives"

17. Which would you rather watch?
    a. The six o'clock news
    b. A TV evangelist

18. Which would you rather read?
    a. The Bible
    b. A Stephen King novel

19. Which would you rather read?
    a. *Campus Life*
    b. *Seventeen*

20. Which would you rather read?
    a. A comic book
    b. A fund-raising letter from TV evangelists

Diagnosis

1. Total the number of a. answers you circled, multiply the sum by two, and write this number on the left side of the slash below.
2. Total the number of b. answers you circled, multiply the sum by two, and write this number on the right side of the slash below.

_____ / _____

Refer to the chart to receive your diagnosis and treatment.

SCORE	DIAGNOSIS	TREATMENT
40/0 38/2 36/4 34/6	**Heavenly vision.** Blessed are your eyes…For I tell you the truth, many prophets and righteous men longed to see what you see but did not see it. (Matt. 13:16-17)	To keep your spiritual vision clear, apply 2 Corinthians 4:16-18.
32/8 30/10 28/12 26/14	**Spiritual farsightedness.** Your eyes are good; therefore you are full of light. Yet because you are farsighted, you overlook the kingdom of God when it is near (see Matt. 6:22).	To correct farsightedness, apply Mark 1:15.
24/16 22/18 20/20 18/22 16/24	**Laodicean vision.** Your eyes are neither good nor bad, neither farsighted nor nearsighted. You therefore run the risk of losing your sight altogether (see Rev. 3:14-16).	Apply Revelation 3:17-18 immediately.
14/26 12/28 10/30 8/32	**Roamin' eyes.** Your eyes have been darkened because they have roamed from the things of God to the passions of this world (see Rom. 11:8-10).	Apply 2 Peter 1:5-9 three times a day.
6/34 4/36 2/38 0/40	**Spiritual glaucoma.** You're just plain blind—spiritually, that is. Your eyes are shot, and the darkness of this world is all around you (see 1 John 2:9-11 and Matt. 6:23).	Your only hope is Jesus' advice in Matthew 5:29.

The Island Affair

The two circles represent two islands that are surrounded by shark-infested waters. After a shipwreck nearby, five survivors manage to reach the safety of the islands. Albert ends up on one island and is separated from his fiancée, Carla, who is stranded on the other island with her mother, Della. Bruno, a young man who is about the same age as Albert, ends up on Albert's island. The fifth survivor is an older man, Edgar. He is a loner who is marooned with Carla and Della.

The situation is this: Albert and Carla are deeply in love and are engaged to be married. After two months of being separated and yet in sight of each other on the islands, they desperately long to be joined. But each passing day makes rescue look more hopeless. Carla becomes despondent.

One day while walking around the island, Carla discovers a crude boat that has been hollowed out of an old tree. It looks seaworthy. She discovers that Edgar has just finished making the boat. Carla tells Edgar about her longing to reach Albert, who is on the other island. Meanwhile, Albert calls across the water, pleading with Edgar to let Carla have the boat. Edgar refuses, saying that he made the boat for his own escape and not for her happiness. When Carla continues to plead, Edgar makes a proposal. If Carla will make love to him, he will take her to the other island in his boat. Carla asks for time to consider his proposal, and runs to find her mother, Della.

Carla explains to her mother that rescue looks hopeless and that if they are to be stranded on an island she should at least be with the person she loves. Della listens sympathetically. After much thought, she gives her advice. "I know you sincerely love Albert and I understand your desire to be with him. But I am afraid the cost is a bit high. It is up to you to do what you want, but my advice would be to wait a bit longer. I'm sure a better solution will come along. Then you will be glad you waited."

Carla considers her mother's advice for a number of days. Finally, she decided to accept Edgar's offer. Carla makes love to Edgar. Edgar keeps his part of the bargain and rows Carla to Albert's island. Albert and Carla embrace and are very happy. But during the day's conversation, Carla recounts for Albert the situation that drove her to strike a bargain with Edgar. She confesses that she made love to Edgar, but only because she loved Albert so much. Albert is deeply hurt. He tries to understand, but finally tells Carla that although he loves her very much, he could not continue their relationship knowing that she had made love to another man. Carla tries to change Albert's mind, but to no avail.

While this discussion is going on, Bruno is listening from behind some bushes. When Albert leaves, Bruno tells Carla that he thinks what she did was admirable. He understands that she made love to Edgar out of desperation; that it was an act of love for Albert. Bruno tells Carla that he would readily accept someone who would pay such a high price for their love and that he would be willing to care for Carla in spite of what Albert did. Carla accepts him.

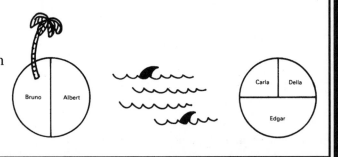

squares. The blue square represents total disagreement, and the red square represents total agreement. The other shades are in between. In other words, if someone felt undecided on the topic, but leaned a little toward the agreement side, then he or she might stand on the yellow-green square. After everyone has chosen a place to stand, ask them to share why they feel as they do.

During the discussion, kids may want to move to a different square, which is perfectly acceptable. If everyone agrees, then you'll have the entire group standing on one of the squares, but this is not your goal. The goal is first of all to allow kids the opportunity to think through some of their values, and then to see them in relationship to the values of others.

WISDOM

WISDOM TEST

Here is an interesting discussion starter on the subject of wisdom based on Proverbs 7-9. Give each of the kids in your group a copy of the survey on page 169, and after they all have completed it, discuss each of the questions in depth. *Dan Mutschler*

GLOBAL PROVERBS

Does your teaching calendar call for a discussion on world missions? Or on wisdom? Or do you need a lively introduction to a study of the book of Proverbs? Give your students copies of Global Proverbs on page 170.

Here are the answers:
• Habits are first cobwebs, **then cables.**
• God save you from a bad neighbor and from **a beginner on the fiddle.**
• A trout in the pot is better than **a salmon in the sea.**
• Before you marry, keep your two eyes open: **after you marry, shut one.**
• Even a small star shines **in the darkness.**
• Beauty in a woman without good judgment is like **a gold ring in a pig's snout.**
• He who cannot dance puts the blame **on the floor.**

• That which is brief, if it be good, is **good twice over.**
• You always find something **the last place you look.**
• If you want your dreams to come true, **don't sleep.**
• Faults are thick where **love is thin.**
• With time and patience the mulberry leaf **becomes a silk gown.**
• Too many captains may steer a boat **up a mountainside.**
• Treat your guest as a guest for two days; **on the third day, give him a hoe.**

Keith Curran

WORRY

WHAT? ME WORRY?

Worry is something we all do. The handout on page 171 is a stimulating outline for a discussion on worry.

WORRY: AN OBJECT LESSON

Use three balloons to illustrate the difference between worry and healthy concern, and how we should deal with worry.

Begin with a deflated balloon in your hand. Tell the group you're going to use it to show the difference between worry and concern. Inflate the balloon about half full, and explain that concern is like this half-inflated balloon. Being concerned means we give over a portion of our time, energy, and thought to deal with a particular situation. What makes this response concern rather than worry is that we can do something about the problem facing us, which is illustrated by deflating the balloon. Dealing with situations frees us for other things.

Explain now that worry, on the other hand, is when we spend our time and energy concentrating on things we really can't change. Inflate the balloon fully and hold it in front of you. When we concentrate on such unchangeable situations, our lives become more and more crowded and tense, until finally we burst (pop the balloon). Ask the

Wisdom Test

1. My friends and family generally consider me to be...
   a. a foolish person
   b. lacking common sense
   c. a "wise guy"
   d. able to make fairly wise decisions except when it comes to _____
   e. wiser than most people
   f. one of the wisest people in the world

2. I consider myself to be...
   a. a foolish person
   b. lacking common sense
   c. a "wise guy"
   d. able to make fairly wise decisions except when it comes to _____
   e. wiser than most people
   f. one of the wisest people in the world

3. I can be talked into things...
   a. always or almost always
   b. often even when I know it is a foolish decision
   c. only when I really wanted it in the first place
   d. sometimes when I see new information
   e. only when physical violence accompanies the talk
   f. never

4. My wisest actions have...
   a. resulted in benefits even others can see
   b. brought about changes only I can appreciate
   c. are still foolish when compared with the actions of most people
   d. are just about like everyone else's wisest actions
   e. are wiser than those of anyone else I know

5. When I'm criticized, I generally...
   a. punch out the person who criticized me
   b. react by screaming and yelling
   c. pout and try to make the person who criticized me feel guilty
   d. ignore the criticism
   e. try to evaluate the criticism honestly and change my ways if I feel it is warranted
   f. appreciate the person who had the guts to share with me and tell him or her so

6. One area where I generally show wisdom in my life is...
   a. money/finances
   b. God
   c. friendships
   d. sex
   e. family
   f. use of time/schedule
   g. food
   h. _____

7. One area where I rarely show wisdom and need drastic improvement is...
   a. money/finances
   b. God
   c. friendships
   d. sex
   e. family
   f. use of time/schedule
   g. food
   h. _____

Global Proverbs

Directions: The following columns list in two parts proverbs from several countries. Choose from the right the correct ending for each proverb, then write that ending on the line.

(Spanish) Habits are first cobwebs,
_____

(Italian) God save you from a bad neighbor and from
_____

(Irish) A trout in the pot is better than
_____

(Jamaican) Before you marry, keep your two eyes open:
_____

(Finnish) Even a small star shines
_____

(Bible) Beauty in a woman without good judgment is like
_____

(Hindi) He who cannot dance puts the blame
_____

(Spanish) That which is brief, if it be good, is
_____

(American) You always find something
_____

(Yiddish) If you want your dreams to come true,
_____

(British) Faults are thick where
_____

(Chinese) With time and patience the mulberry leaf
_____

(Korean) Too many captains may steer a boat
_____

(Swahili) Treat your guest as a guest for two days;
_____

in the darkness.

becomes a silk gown.

love is thin.

on the floor.

up a mountainside.

don't sleep.

on the third day, give him a hoe.

a gold ring in a pig's snout.

after you marry, shut one.

then cables.

a beginner on the fiddle.

the last place you look.

good twice over.

a salmon in the sea.

WHAT? ME WORRY?

1. Respond to these statements:
   - Christians should never worry._____
   _____

   - Why worry? _____
   _____

   - If you don't care enough to worry, you don't care. _____
   _____

2. List some things that you worry about. _____
   _____

3. List some things that your parents worry about. _____
   _____

4. Can you list any good consequences of worrying?_____
   _____

5. Can you list any bad consequences of worrying? _____
   _____

6. What would you say to someone who was worried about:
   - His parents getting a divorce? _____
   - Failing in school? _____
   - Unconfessed sin? _____
   - The recent loss of a boyfriend/girlfriend? _____
   - Future plans?_____
   - A bad case of acne? _____
   - A meaningless prayer life? _____
   - A recent failure? _____
   - Death?_____
   - Being pregnant and unmarried? _____

kids for examples of things people become worried about but can't change.

Next, take a second balloon and inflate it less than half full. Hold it in front of you and poke it with your finger, allowing the surface of the balloon to contract and expand. Explain that when we concentrate only on those things we can change, instead of fretting over unchangeables, we're more flexible and less sensitive to other pressures. Inflate the balloon fully and tell the kids that a life filled with pointless worry makes us less able to deal with other pressures that come our way, and can cause even small problems to explode emotionally (pop the balloon). Ask the kids for examples of times when they or others they know have overreacted to some small irritation or pressure because they were already worried about something.

Finally, take a third balloon and tell the kids that some things happen in life that cause us a great deal of concern—things we can't change, but wish we could, such as the death of a friend or a divorce in the family. Explain that often during such times people are full of fear or anger or confusion. Inflate the balloon and ask the kids what they can do in a situation like that. Tell them that God has something to say about that situation, and about all the times when they're tempted to worry. Read or quote Philippians 4:6-7. Assure them that God will help them deal with their worries and concerns and will give them his peace. Let the balloon go so that it flies around the room until it's deflated.

For added emphasis, make sure you take your time inflating the balloons and popping them. Some of the kids will slightly dread the pop, which is a form of worry. *Joe Harvey*

172

YOUTH SPECIALTIES TITLES

Professional Resources

Administration, Publicity, & Fundraising (Ideas Library)

Developing Student Leaders

Equipped to Serve: Volunteer Youth Worker Training Course

Help! I'm a Junior High Youth Worker!

Help! I'm a Sunday School Teacher!

Help! I'm a Volunteer Youth Worker!

How to Expand Your Youth Ministry

How to Speak to Youth...and Keep Them Awake at the Same Time

One Kid at a Time: Reaching Youth through Mentoring

A Youth Ministry Crash Course

The Youth Worker's Handbook to Family Ministry

Youth Ministry Programming

Camps, Retreats, Missions, & Service Ideas (Ideas Library)

Compassionate Kids: Practical Ways to Involve Your Students in Mission and Service

Creative Bible Lessons in John: Encounters with Jesus

Creative Bible Lessons in Romans: Faith on Fire!

Creative Bible Lessons on the Life of Christ

Creative Junior High Programs from A to Z, Vol. 1 (A-M)

Creative Meetings, Bible Lessons, & Worship Ideas (Ideas Library)

Crowd Breakers & Mixers (Ideas Library)

Drama, Skits, & Sketches (Ideas Library)

Dramatic Pauses

Facing Your Future: Graduating Youth Group with a Faith That Lasts

Games (Ideas Library)

Games 2 (Ideas Library)

Great Fundraising Ideas for Youth Groups

Great Retreats for Youth Groups

Greatest Skits on Earth

Greatest Skits on Earth, Vol. 2

Holiday Ideas (Ideas Library)

Hot Illustrations for Youth Talks

Incredible Questionnaires for Youth Ministry

Junior High Game Nights

Kickstarters: 101 Ingenious Intros to Just about Any Bible Lesson

Memory Makers

More Great Fundraising Ideas for Youth Groups

More Hot Illustrations for Youth Talks

More Junior High Game Nights

Play It Again! More Great Games for Groups

Play It! Great Games for Groups

Special Events (Ideas Library)

Spontaneous Melodramas

Super Sketches for Youth Ministry

Teaching the Bible Creatively

Up Close and Personal: How to Build Community in Your Youth Group

Wild Truth Bible Lessons

Worship Services for Youth Groups

Discussion Starter Resources

Discussion & Lesson Starters (Ideas Library)

Discussion & Lesson Starters 2 (Ideas Library)

4th-6th Grade TalkSheets

Get 'Em Talking

High School TalkSheets

High School TalkSheets: Psalms and Proverbs

Junior High TalkSheets

Junior High TalkSheets: Psalms and Proverbs

Keep 'Em Talking!

More High School TalkSheets

More Junior High TalkSheets

What If...? 450 Thought-Provoking Questions to Get Teenagers Talking, Laughing, and Thinking

Would You Rather...? 465 Provocative Questions to Get Teenagers Talking

Clip Art

ArtSource Vol. 1—Fantastic Activities

ArtSource Vol. 2—Borders, Symbols, Holidays, and Attention Getters

ArtSource Vol. 3—Sports

ArtSource Vol. 4—Phrases and Verses

ArtSource Vol. 5—Amazing Oddities and Appalling Images

ArtSource Vol. 6—Spiritual Topics

ArtSource Vol. 7—Variety Pack

ArtSource Vol. 8—Stark Raving Clip Art

ArtSource CD-ROM (contains Vols. 1-7)

Videos

EdgeTV

The Heart of Youth Ministry: A Morning with Mike Yaconelli

Next Time I Fall in Love Video Curriculum

Understanding Your Teenager Video Curriculum

Student Books

Grow For It Journal

Grow For It Journal through the Scriptures

Wild Truth Journal for Junior Highers